Seeing Suffrage

Seeing Suffrage

The Washington Suffrage Parade of 1913, Its Pictures, and Its Effect on the American Political Landscape

James Glen Stovall • Foreword by Edward Caudill

The University of Tennessee Press • Knoxville

The images reproduced in the "The Photographs" section of this book are from the following sources:

Library of Congress: Photographs 1–5, 7, 9–12, 14–19, 21–26, 28–34, 36, 41, 43–44, 52, 55–57, 59–61, 75, 79, 81, 83, 89, 96–98.

The Sewall-Belmont House, Washington, DC: Photographs 6, 8, 13, 20, 27, 35, 37–40, 42, 45–51, 53–54, 58, 62–74, 76–77, 80, 82, 84–88, 90–95. Reproduced with permission.

United States Senate: Photograph 78.

The paper in this book meets the requirements of American National Standards Institute / National Information Standards Organization specification Z39.48–1992 (Permanence of Paper). It contains 30 percent post-consumer waste and is certified by the Forest Stewardship Council.

Library of Congress Cataloging-in-Publication Data

Stovall, James Glen.
Seeing suffrage: the Washington Suffrage Parade of 1913, its pictures, and its effect on the American political landscape / James Glen Stovall; foreword by Edward Caudill. — First edition
    pages cm
Includes bibliographical references and index.
ISBN-13: 978-1-57233-940-8 (hardcover)
ISBN-10: 1-57233-940-3 (hardcover)
 1. Women—Suffrage—United States—History—20th century.
 2. Women—Suffrage—United States—History—20th century—Pictorial works.
 3. Women—Suffrage—Washington (D.C.)—History—20th century.
 4. Women—Suffrage—Washington (D.C.)—History—20th century—Pictorial works.
 5. Processions—Washington (D.C.)—History—20th century.
 6. Processions—Washington (D.C.)—History—20th century—Pictorial works.
 7. Women—Political activity—United States—History—20th century.
 8. United States—Politics and government—20th century.
 I. Title.

JK1896.S83 2013

324.6'230973—dc23   2012032040

Contents

Foreword

The photographs in this book are an extraordinary record of an extraordinary time in the growth of American democracy. When the suffrage parade took place in 1913, the movement was sixty-five years old. It would take another seven years of agitation, arrests, and headlines before passage of the Nineteenth Amendment. These pictures depict a bit of historical realism—history that is messy, a mixture of heroes and knaves, a spectacle in the cause of a great moral issue, an event that was little more than press pandering and mob appeal set to the pursuit of a righteous goal. The mob disrupted the event but helped nurture the cause by making the parade even more newsworthy than it would have been as an orderly, sparsely attended walk through cold streets.

The early twentieth century was an exciting time in American history, a little too exciting for some people, especially those rigidly defending traditions secular and sacred. Change coursed through society, impelled marchers, threatened the entrenched, and heralded promise for the downtrodden. It was an era of reform. The economy was shifting from the family farm to the city and industry. Progressives rode the currents of change and set themselves against the abuses of the Gilded Age and the Robber Barons. The reformers' wildly ambitious goals included government regulation, broader democracy, and public service. Perhaps the biggest idea of all was that government had some responsibility for the welfare of its citizenry, all of them, not just a monied few who had been served so well during the Gilded Age. Progressives pushed for government responsibility for infrastructure, education, health, workplace safety, and even the setting aside of vast tracts of land for conservation instead of exploitation. Those in the suffrage movement understood the new expectations of and role for government, in particular the federal government.

The assault on tradition often met with resistance. The women who challenged convention provoked similar anxiety. The suffrage movement was only one manifestation of a new, emerging culture. The changing role of women in the industrial economy was highlighted during World War I, when the number of women in the workforce surged. Public education was growing, for men and women, providing new opportunities and roles for all. New modes of communication were eroding old barriers, physical and intellectual, to new ideas. Two machines of the new era of communications, the telephone and the typewriter, meant new opportunities for women outside the home. These new ideas, new technology, and new social roles were not mere adjustments to the status quo. These changes were altering individuals' places in the home, in the workplace, and giving rise to new voices in and models for the structure of society.

Society needed changing, according to a group of journalists who often provided the first glimpse of societal ills and injustice. Muckraker Jacob Riis revealed the filth of slum life in *How the Other Half Lives* (1890) and *The Battle with the Slum* (1902). Lincoln Steffens bared municipal corruption with *The Shame of the Cities* (1904), which began as a series of articles in *McClure's Magazine*. Ida Tarbell charted the excesses of monopoly in her *History of the Standard Oil Company* (1904), which also began in *McClure's*. David Graham Phillips's *The Treason of the Senate* (1906) exposed the corrupt influence of special interests over state legislators, who at the time still elected U.S. senators. Phillips's work was a major force in the eventual passage of the Seventeenth Amendment, which authorized direct election of U.S. senators by the voters. Upton Sinclair, in *The Jungle* (1906), intended to provoke sympathy for labor but instead incited indignation over the foul conditions at meat-packing plants. The work provoked governmental oversight of the food and drug producers. Those muckraker raids were part of the larger battle to reform and expand democracy, not just in terms of suffrage but also with respect to economic justice, regulation of monopolies, health and safety standards, and having elected officials answer to the electorate rather than a party machine.

Just as democracy was beginning to embrace more people, so was the press. Part of that wider appeal was visual, with introduction of technology that allowed inexpensive reproduction of pictures in newspapers, and the growth of film as mass entertainment. In the newspaper industry, "mass" media had taken on a new dimension of largesse with the era of Pulitzer, Hearst, and "yellow journalism." Mass circulation meant mass appeal, which often meant news adorned with sensation, enhanced by photographs.

Attuned to the journalism of the era, the suffragists demonstrated a good sense of mixing substance with spectacle. The parade energized a movement that had been in the doldrums for nearly two decades. The Washington suffrage parade was a lesson for suffragists, who discovered the now-clichéd axiom that all publicity is good publicity. Four years later, the suffragists picketed the White House, provoking their own arrests, and feeding the news machine even further by going on a hunger strike in prison.

The photos in this volume say something about the complexity of the logistics of the event and the response to it, providing a glimpse into creating news in the service of a cause. The suffragists are striking figures, forcefully making their way through the often hostile crowds at the center of the nation's capital. The parade was a metaphor for a new chapter in democracy, which again would be acted out on the streets before enacted in the Congress, trudging through mobs before winding through legislatures. The pictures show something historic not just in its inherent significance, but in the machinations of democracy—a lofty ideal paraded along unruly streets.

Edward Caudill

Preface

The Washington suffrage parade of March 3, 1913—officially titled by its creators as the Woman Suffrage Procession—spanned but a brief moment in the history of the debate over whether women in the United States should vote. On that day, no one understood or could have predicted the outcome or the broader implications of the events.

Alice Paul, the woman who set these events in motion, envisioned an event that would arrest and impress viewers with a kaleidoscope of color, people, and ideas. Grace, movement, and feminine beauty would be the tools that would lift the idea of suffrage onto a higher plane of public debate than it had ever attained in the United States. There were stirrings in this new century that made the timing right for such an event. Paul understood all this as well as anyone of her age, and she acted with a fierce determination, and against monumental odds, to make it happen.

But not even Paul could have foreseen the broader effects of the parade, and she certainly could not have predicted the outcome of the events of that day.

Paul's immediate goal was to have both men and women see and take seriously the idea of an amendment to the U.S. Constitution that would allow women to vote. To that end, Paul succeeded beyond any reasonable measure. Although it took seven years of difficult and frustrating political work to ratify the Nineteenth Amendment, the parade can rightly be seen as the moment when everything about the suffrage debate changed.

The changes that the Nineteenth Amendment wrought were subtle and profound and are still being felt a century after its passage. In the continuing debate over who has power in America—a debate that has been going on since

Europeans first landed on the continent—the Nineteenth Amendment represented the single most radical and extensive broadening of the electorate in our history. This shift ultimately affected every corner of political life.

So, looking at the parade and its subsequent events after a century can tell us much about the place and the era in which it happened, about the attitudes of Americans at the beginning of the modern age, and about the way journalism had changed.

And look—literally—we can.

The event was created in great part for pictures. It was one of the first political events in American history that was staged for visual purposes. Fortunately, many of those photographs taken that day have survived. This book showcases the most interesting and informative pictures of that day and presents the people who participated in it. If we look at these photos closely, they will reveal much about the people of the time and about ourselves.

This book exists because my friend and colleague Ed Caudill recognized its possibilities. Ed is a historian and scholar of the first order and a specialist in the political ideas of the early twentieth century. When I described the Washington parade and the pictures I had discovered in the process of doing some general research on women's suffrage, he said, "There's your book. That's the one you should do first."

Ed then told me to call Scot Danforth, director of the University of Tennessee Press, to see if he would be interested. When I finally got around to doing that, Scot was open and soon enthusiastic about the project.

So, I owe much to Ed for giving me the idea. And, since no good deed should go unpunished, I asked Ed to write a foreword to the book. He kindly consented to do so, and his piece sets this event into a larger context that helps the reader understand its implications.

Thanks should go also to Scot Danforth for his interest in this project and his efforts in seeing it through from creation to publication.

The two people who formally reviewed the manuscript—Janice Hume of the University of Georgia and Kris Myers of the Alice Paul Institute—were enormously helpful with their ideas, information, corrections, and suggestions. They made this a better book, and I thank them very much.

Special thanks is also due to Jennifer Krafchik, assistant director and director of collections at the Sewall-Belmont House in Washington, D.C. Jennifer generously made all of the pictures of the suffrage parade in the Sewell-Belmont collection available for this book. She spent much time and effort in reading the manuscript, responding to my inquiries, and making suggestions. She has been a willing and contributing partner throughout this project, and her efforts have made this book a richer experience for the readers. I am humbly grateful to her.

My daughter-in-law Francoise Stovall read an early version of the manuscript and made many helpful comments. My wife, Sally, who gives an intelligent reading to most everything I write, suffered nobly through yet another book manuscript, and I am always grateful to her and my son Jeff for their encouragement and support.

None of these good people, of course, is responsible for any shortcomings in this work. That responsibility is mine alone.

The 1913 Washington Suffrage Parade

Jane Burleson glanced at her wristwatch as she sat, ramrod straight, on her horse. The seconds, then the minutes, were ticking away. Burleson was an impressive figure. Tall, beautiful, regal. In command. Behind her was Inez Milholland, dressed in a white flowing gown and seated on a light-colored horse named "Grey Dawn." Milholland had been designated by the press as the "most beautiful suffragist." When she passed in front of the crowd, you couldn't help but look.

But Burleson led the parade. She was the grand marshal. She was the one the crowd would see first. Her watch ticked relentlessly on. It was after three o'clock. The parade should have already started, and she was supposed to start it. But the signal hadn't arrived.

Burleson gazed around. What she was seeing did not please her. Lots of people were milling about. The day was clear and crisp, slightly cool but not uncomfortable. That part was fine, but there was too much disorder. She was used to military parades. The wife of an Army officer, she knew how these things were supposed to happen.

Where was the signal?

She looked around again. In front of her was the Peace Monument, the official beginning of the parade. To her right was the U.S. Capitol Building, dominating the eastern horizon. Behind her were at least five thousand marchers, along with bands, floats, horses. They were waiting on her. She knew that, if they didn't move soon, whatever order was left would dissipate.

She saw a policeman standing nearby and asked him to see that the lines of marchers behind her closed up.

He scowled at her and said something she couldn't hear. He didn't move.

She asked again, commanded even. He did nothing.

As a society woman, as the wife of an army lieutenant, she was used to giving orders. She was used to being obeyed. Besides, Richard Sylvester, chief of the Washington police, had told her that his force was at her command. All she had to do was tell them what she wanted.

She invoked Sylvester's name. It did no good.

"I will not budge from here," he said. "I have my orders."

"I am going to report you to Major Sylvester for insolence and impudence, for he said you were to obey my orders."

"Report—oh, oh, go ahead and report," he said and turned away from her.

Bystanders who heard the exchange began to hoot and shout. Clearly, they were with the policeman and didn't mind seeing a bossy woman get her comeuppance. Burleson turned her horse and rode away. It was not a good start, and things would get worse.[1]

Inez Milholland had been here before. She was no stranger to crowds, parades, and photographers. She was the star of the show, as she had been for two previous suffrage parades in New York City. As she had been the night before at the

Columbia Theatre in Washington when she spoke to the packed auditorium and helped raise five thousand dollars—nearly 40 percent of the entire expenses of the parade—for Alice Paul's congressional committee.

Now at the base of the U.S. Capitol Building in Washington, D.C., in flowing white robes on a light-colored horse, she attracted a small crowd of her own, mostly men.

Her long flowing dark curls contrasted sharply with her white gown. She had been told to wear yellow, one of the parade's official colors. But white was her color, and that's what she wore.[2]

Milholland knew her value as a symbol, but she was more than that. She had more suffrage experience than most of the women around her. At Vassar she had organized suffrage meetings expressly against the wishes of the administration. In London, she had spoken at the first outdoor suffrage march. In New York she had participated in garment worker strikes and rallies.

And, just three days before, she learned that she had passed the New York bar exam and could now practice law. She looked forward to using her skills to advance the cause of social justice.

But today, she was a symbol—a role assigned to her by Alice Paul. It was Alice's show, and Milholland was glad to be the star.

Alice Paul could not enjoy the day or feel much sense of triumph. There was simply too much to do—too much to see about, too many questions to answer, too many problems to be fixed.

Now it was past three o'clock.

Some things wouldn't get done. It was time for her to climb into a car that would be part of the beginning of the parade.

Still, she must have felt some sense of satisfaction as she looked around. She could see the colors—green, yellow, purple, white. She could see, in her mind's eye, what was about to take place a mile and a quarter away on the plaza of the U.S. Treasury building.

It would be a pageant—a tableau—of unsurpassed beauty and grace, professionally produced and dazzling in its visual effect.

And as the pageant unfolded, thousands of women would be marching by, women from every walk of life, from every part of the nation. The entire afternoon would be one that no one could ignore. The thousands of people who saw it would never forget this day.

Alice Paul knew that the nation had to see suffrage. People had to get the idea of women voting in their heads. She had chosen the time and the stage—the nation's capital city on the day before the inauguration of a new president.

Three months before, all this had simply been an idea held by Alice Paul and a few of her companions. Now it was about to happen.[3]

Patience Ceased to Be a Virtue

By the end of the first decade of the twentieth century, proponents of women's suffrage could claim only a few small victories. Women's suffrage had been part of the Women's Rights Conference in Seneca Falls, New York, in 1848—and the only part of the conference proposals that engendered serious debate. That debate had been going on for sixty-five years. Could women be full participants in the political realm, maintain a proper home, and raise children as society needed them? Many people still thought the answer was no.

Most of those first suffragists at Seneca Falls were part of, or sympathetic to, the abolitionist movement. Freeing America from slavery, not suffrage, would be the great reformist crusade of the next fifteen years.

Still, people such as Elizabeth Cady Stanton and Susan B. Anthony had reason to hope that, once the slaves were free, women would be ushered into full citizenship along with America's newly freed citizens. They believed women had earned that privilege through their work for abolition. Those hopes were shattered by the political realities of post–Civil War America when debate on the Fifteenth Amendment began in 1869. The amendment read, "The right of citizens of the United States to vote shall not be denied or abridged by the United States or by any state on account of race, color, or previous condition of servitude."

Stanton, Anthony, and others argued vehemently that the word "sex" also should be a condition that could not deny citizens the right to vote, but the political will to include so radical a proposal did not exist. Even Frederick Douglass, who had worked so closely with many of the suffragists, did not stand by these women. He was willing to take just half a loaf—the half that gave African American men the right to vote. For the next forty years, suffragists fought

FEMALE LONGEVITY.

[New York Press.]

Women are living longer than they did 25 years ago, but the doctors aren't agreed on the reason. Though all admit it isn't due to the spread of the suffrage movement, they are widely divided in their opinions about it. Statistics compiled in England show that the expectation of life of a woman of 50 is a year greater than it was in 1875, while that of a man is only a few months greater. One school of doctors, who believe that death is due entirely to a wearing out of brain tissues, says the greater longevity of women is due to the fact that they don't use their brains as much as men. On the other side of the scientific fence is a group of doctors who insist woman lives longer now because she is more sheltered than man; doesn't have to face the wearing competition of business that he has to endure and that she spends most of her time at home, which is more airy and healthful than the offices where men work.

The idea of suffrage was taken lightly by newspaper editors, as females often were generally. This item appeared in the *Washington Post* on December 29, 1912, two months before the Washington Suffrage Parade. (Courtesy of the *Washington Post*.)

apathy, entrenched beliefs, ridicule, and sometimes each other. A suffrage amendment was proposed in Congress, occasionally debated, rarely reported to the floor of one house or the other, and always voted down.

Suffragists retreated to the states and took their victories where they could find them. By 1896, four western states—Wyoming, Utah, Colorado, and Idaho—had granted women the right to vote. With those victories, the major suffrage organization, the National American Woman Suffrage Association (NAWSA), had developed a strategy that concentrated on persuading states to hold referenda on women's suffrage and then trying the cajole men into voting for it. The arguments against suffrage could be easily made, however, and even in statewide campaigns suffragists lost many more times than they won.

By the turn of the century, NAWSA had become a large, ineffective organization of mostly white middle- and upper-class women. Local NAWSA groups bickered with one another, and the national organization was so democratically oriented that almost every important proposal needed a near consensus to be implemented. NAWSA could not develop a plan that gave members much hope of achieving any national victory. So focused was NAWSA on its state-by-state strategy that the idea of a federal amendment was almost completely ignored.

Much of the thinking about suffrage during that time is reflected in President William Howard Taft's welcoming speech to the NAWSA's national convention in Washington in 1910. Taft was opposed to suffrage and did not sugar-coat that opposition even in front of that group. He favored suffrage once, he said, when he was sixteen years old. He had since thought about it and become opposed. "The theory that Hottentots or any other uneducated, altogether unintelligent class is fitted for self-government at once or to take part in government is a theory that I wholly dissent from." Some of the women in the room hissed at those remarks, a clear insult to the president. He continued, however, "Now, my dear ladies, you must show yourselves equal to self government by exercising, in listening to opposing argument, that degree of restraint without which self-government is impossible." NAWSA President Anna Howard Shaw was mortified—not at the president but at her membership. The next day she led the convention in a vote to send a letter of regret to the White House.

The hissing by some of the conventioneers was the focus of the *Washington Post*'s report with the headline, TAFT IS HISSED BY SUFFRAGISTS: "The President of the United States, although a guest of honor, was hissed last evening at the Arlington Hotel in the convention of the National American Woman Suffrage Association, for exercising his right to free speech." The article continued in a sympathetic vein to the insulted president, at one point referring to "his overanxious listeners [who] forgot their manners."[4]

Outrageous as the president's remarks may seem to twenty-first-century readers, the incident exemplifies the low regard that suffrage and suffragists—and women in general—had in the eyes of men of the time. With regard to political and public issues, women were seen as immature. Better they should stay at home and raise the children. Women who agitated in public for suffrage must be unhappy or unhinged or unnatural—or perhaps all three.

Despite that, the environment for acceptance of the idea of women's suffrage was shifting in significant and fundamental ways. Three of those shifts—the increasing power of the federal government, the changes in daily journalism, and the expanding roles for women in society—were to have profound effects on the upcoming battle for suffrage.

The Increased Power and Presence of the Federal Government

In the decades following the Civil War, states reasserted themselves as the major components of political life. The series of Republicans (and one Democrat, Grover Cleveland) who occupied the White House during that time showed little inclination to do anything other than have the federal government stay small, inexpensive, and out of the way.

This was particularly true in the area of voting. After the passage of the Fifteenth Amendment, Washington had little to do with who and how people voted. Whites, especially in southern states, were determined to reclaim their state capitals after what they viewed as the horror and lawlessness of Reconstruction. By the 1890s southerners began systematically excluding blacks from the voting booth while keeping a wary eye out for anything that might induce interference from Washington.

The inevitable backlash to increased state power occurred when the Progressive movement saw national government as a solution to corruption of state governments. Solutions and reforms that Progressives identified control of interstate monopolies, cleaning up state legislatures, direct election of senators, labor legislation, and consumer protection, to name a few—had to be undertaken nationally. Into this milieu stepped Theodore Roosevelt, who, although a Republican, was no shrinking violet when it came to exercising and expanding the power of the federal government.

Women reformers—not necessarily suffragists—recognized the power and efficiency with which reforms could be enacted if done on a federal level. Women had an interest in strengthening the home (often through prohibition), reforming municipal and state governments, increasing child welfare services, and building better school systems, among other issues. Taking on these issues at a local level was exceeding difficult and frustrating, and the reforms achieved at one moment could be undone at the next election. Reforms at the federal level could be efficiently focused, widely distributed, and permanent.

Woodrow Wilson's election promised to continue this trend. In 1913 Wilson was assuming office on a reform platform that vowed to solve problems—certain problems, at least—at a national level. He was the opposite of Roosevelt in personality and personal outlook (and the two despised each other), but in their own ways both viewed Washington as the instrument of solutions.[5]

These political changes took years to develop and were not readily visible to everyone, but they were real, and they were rendering NAWSA's state-by-state strategy increasingly irrelevant.

Changes in Journalism

Journalism changes most profoundly and most quickly in response to two factors: audience and technology. The daily journalism that emerged from the late 1890s into the early years of the twentieth century was produced by a group of editors and reporters decidedly different from the ones who had worked in the business just two decades earlier. They had different tools and were serving a different audience. The profession had passed through the era of "yellow journalism" with its excesses of sensationalism but also with the instructive power of how to write a story that was interesting to a mass audience.

By 1913 journalism had also seen the rise of the "muckrakers" and the power that information—faithfully gathered and carefully constructed—could wield in a modernizing society. The investigative journalism of the decade had provoked the federal government into passing measures such as the Hepburn Act of 1905 authorizing the Interstate Commerce Commission to tighten controls on railroads; the Meat Inspection Act of 1906; the Pure Food and Drug Act of 1907; and the Mann Act of 1909 which prohibited the transportation of females across state lines for immoral purposes. Each of these pieces of legislation came from the efforts of journalists to expose practices and conditions that most of their readers would deem wrong or unworthy of American society.[6]

Reporters and editors had backed away from the "journalism of action" that characterized much of the 1890s. Increasingly professional and somewhat more dispassionate, journalists saw their job as presenting information rather than righting wrongs. More and more, they were taking themselves out of the story and letting the information and characters they wrote about command the drama. The journalist's job was to select and shape the information. There needed to be a narrative form, even if it wasn't chronological. There needed to characters and conflict to hold the interest of readers.

An important technological development that supplemented this reporting was the use of photographs in the production of the day's news. Despite the existence and popularity of photography well before the Civil War, there was no efficient way of printing photographs until the development of a half-toning process in the 1880s. Even then, it took more than a decade to achieve good photo quality from a large, high-speed press. That finally happened in 1897.

The technology of mass-producing photographs helped mitigate the cultural war that was going on within journalism at the time over the appropriateness of photos themselves within a news context. Many reporters and editors believed that photos could not—and should not—replace words. Photography sensationalized the news and distracted readers from the important information and explanation carried by text. In 1893, the *Nation* magazine called the use of photographs in news publications "infantile."[7]

By 1913, photographs had become a central part of journalism's daily fare. They were a relatively easy way to fill space on the pages, and there was a built-in accuracy to them. Pictures didn't lie, or so the thinking went.[8] Photography, according to photojournalism historian Michael Carleback, made coverage of news events "more sophisticated and far more effective."[9]

It was an increasingly visual age. Readers expected to see the stories as well as to read them. Newspapers hired their own photographers, bought freelanced pictures, and purchased them from services set up for that purpose. Three of those services were the Bain News Service (established in 1898), Harris and Ewing (1905) and the National Photo Company (about 1909). They found plenty of eager clients among the newspapers of the day.[10]

The 1913 Washington Suffrage Parade

The Flow of Women into the Workforce

The early twentieth century was a time of limited but expanding opportunities for women. In the previous decades, women had essentially two choices for their lives: marriage and domesticity or teaching and spinsterhood. The former was by far more financially secure, but it was unsatisfactory to a growing number of women who were discovering the benefits of education and independence.

In 1890, the number of bachelor's degrees awarded to women was 2,682. By 1900, that number had doubled to 5,237, and it took another jump in 1910 to 8,437. These numbers and the accumulation of women who had college degrees are tiny compared to the entire population of the United States (about 92 million in 1910), but they are important in understanding the undercurrents of the suffrage movement.[11] Many other women were entering teaching and non-teaching jobs without college degrees, of course. Journalism itself was one of the earliest "professions" that was open to women. The typewriter and telephone had created a clerical profession to which women, in the eyes of their male bosses, were particularly well suited.

Some of these women—those who were choosing life outside the home—were drawn to the cause of suffrage, believing that it was a logical step toward expanding their options.[12] They were not inclined to be content with strictly proscribed political rights or with the "give no offense" policy of NAWSA. They were more likely to align with feminist writer and suffragist Charlotte Perkins Gilman, who said, "There was a time when Patience ceased to be a virtue. It was long ago."

Alice Paul was one of these women.

Deeds, Not Words

WON'T TRY TO START SUFFRAGE WAR HERE.

The *New York Times* headline on January 2, 1910, topped the story of a young American woman in London who had joined the suffrage movement there, taken part in demonstrations, gotten herself arrested, participated in a hunger strike, and had been subjected to forced feeding while in Holloway Prison. She was on her way home. Once there, she said, she did not intend to take part in the suffrage movement in the United States. She also commented that the suffrage movement in America was in the "ridicule" stage.[13]

That young woman was Alice Paul. Before going to England in 1907, Paul had not shown much interest in suffrage. She grew up in a well-to-do Quaker family on a farm in New Jersey and in 1901 entered Swarthmore College. She graduated in 1905 and continued her studies, concentrating in social work—one of the few non-teaching professions open to women—at the University of Pennsylvania. She obtained her master's degree in 1907 and received a fellowship to study in England that year.

Working at the Woodbrooke Settlement House in Birmingham, Paul saw Christabel Pankhurst attempt to give a speech on the street one day, only to be heckled off her podium and escorted to safety by police. Paul introduced herself to Pankhurst, who invited her to join the Women's Social and Political Union along with Pankhurst's sister Sylvia and mother, Emmeline. Paul was impressed by the boldness and passion of these women as well as the tactics they were using.

Unlike their American counterparts, these suffragists—known derisively as "suffragettes"—made a lot of noise and news by confronting members of the government over their intransigence on women's suffrage. Their motto was "Deeds, Not Words." Their strategy was to hold the party in power responsible for their not having the right to vote. In

LONDON — ARREST OF A SUFFRAGETTE

June 1908, they held a giant parade in London in which thousands of women (as many as 30,000 by one estimate) walked through the streets in support of the idea of women having the vote. They converged in Hyde Park, where there was a crowd of more than 250,000 waiting to see and participate. One of those marching was Paul.[14]

That fall, Paul moved to London to enter the London School of Economics for work on yet another degree. The move brought her closer to the center of the work of the WSPU. She attended meetings, sold newspapers, and participated in

Much of the news about suffrage was coming from Great Britain, where militant suffragists (known derisively as "suffragettes") were making a spectacle of themselves and often getting arrested. The leader of these militants was Emmeline Pankhurst, shown here getting hauled away by a couple of burly bobbies. Pankhurst's approach to suffrage had immense influence on many American suffragists, including Alice Paul and Lucy Burns. (Library of Congress.)

ardent discussions about tactics and goals. Just standing on the street trying to sell suffrage literature was an education to Paul. The venue was dirty, and the treatment she received from passers-by generally vile. Yet, these conditions emboldened rather than depressed those suffragists with whom she was working.

This cauldron of passion and activity fueled her own feelings about women's rights. She became more active and committed and more willing to join the suffragists in increasingly dangerous activities. In June 1909 she was arrested with a group of women led by Emmeline Pankhurst trying to enter the House of Parliament. At the police station, she met another American, Lucy Burns, a Vassar graduate from Brooklyn who had been doing postgraduate work in Germany. Burns had come to England specifically to participate in the demonstration.

A series of arrests that summer established a strategy for the British suffragists. They would be arrested and demand status as political prisoners. When refused, they would go on a hunger strike. That would provoke authorities into force-feeding to make sure that the suffragists did not die in their custody and become martyrs. But it also generated enormous publicity for the suffragists, both in England and in America, and put those in power on the defensive.

MISS PAUL DESCRIBES FEEDING BY FORCE

American Suffragette in Holloway Jail Lay Abed During Whole of 30-Day Sentence.

REFUSED PRISON CLOTHES

Three Wardresses and Two Doctors Held Her While Food Was Injected Through Nostrils—Now Released.

Special Cable to THE NEW YORK TIMES.

LONDON, Dec. 9.—Miss Alice Paul of Philadelphia, the suffragette who was arrested Nov. 9 and sentenced to a month's hard labor for her share in the suffragette demonstration at the Lord Mayor's banquet at the Guildhall, was released from Holloway Jail this morning on the completion of her thirty days. She left the prison in a cab, ac-

When Alice Paul returned to America after her stint in Great Britain, she was a celebrity because of her arrests, imprisonment, and force-feedings. She had many opportunities to tell her story, as reported here in the *New York Times* in December 1909. (Courtesy of the *New York Times*.)

American journalists and editors noted in particular that two young American women, Paul and Burns, were full participants in all of these events. By the end of the year, both had been arrested on several occasions, had gone on hunger strikes, and had been force-fed. By the time Paul returned home in January 1910, she had some status as a celebrity and was met by reporters in Philadelphia when her boat docked.

Paul's fame provided her with several speaking engagements over the next few months, including a place on the 1910 NAWSA program in Washington (the same one where President Taft referred to the women as "Hottentots"). She discussed her experiences in England and described in detail being held down and force-fed. The influence of Emmeline Pankhurst's approach to gaining broader rights for women was seeping into the American suffrage psyche. Paul was just one of several American women influenced by Pankhurst. In addition, news accounts of what the suffragettes were doing in England were a favorite topic of American editors. British suffragists were not asking for suffrage. They were *demanding* it.[15]

Paul was not ready to start the "suffrage war" that journalists might have hoped for, however. She had another degree to pursue—this one a doctorate in economics from the University of Pennsylvania. But she could not keep herself away from the suffrage movement, especially after she had made contact with some Philadelphia suffragists who were willing to try something new. Paul helped organize street meetings in 1911. These meetings featured women speaking from a platform to anyone who would stop and listen—an almost unthinkable concept for the time. The meetings introduced Paul's cohorts to the dangers and exhilarations of public speaking and to the bonds that can form when individuals face treacherous situations together.

Lucy Burns's return to the United States provided Paul with a companion with whom she had shared experiences. Like Paul, Burns fully understood the strategy they needed to develop to promote suffrage in America. Burns was a fiery redhead, a Catholic, and a fearless crusader. Paul was calm, steady, and rarely seemed flustered. Despite the differences in temperament and background, she and Paul became perfectly aligned in their thinking about how to turn the suffrage movement in America in a different direction.

Mutually supportive, they decided to approach the NAWSA leadership with an idea.

A Foot in the Door

Their first approach didn't go well.

Paul and Burns shopped their ideas around at the 1912 NAWSA national conference in Philadelphia that November, asking to be put in charge of the Congressional Committee, the Washington arm of the organization. Exactly what they said and to whom are not clear, but their proposal to emphasize a federal suffrage amendment met stiff resistance. The NAWSA leadership wanted nothing to do with any real efforts to work at the national level. The leadership certainly was not ready to take on the Democratic Party—big winners in the elections earlier that month—and hold it responsible for the plight of women's suffrage. Many in NAWSA were still irritated with Jane Addams for endorsing Theodore Roosevelt and the Bull Moose Party because of the party's pledge to support women's suffrage. A basic tenant of NAWSA was to be nonpartisan. Addams had abandoned that principle, and Roosevelt still lost. Look where that got us, they were saying.

But Jane Addams was the key. She was the one person, Paul and Burns believed, within the leadership who could get them inside NAWSA. Addams, the founder of the Hull House settlement community in Chicago, listened to the two young women and saw their passion. She also understood the timidity of the organization. She told them she would support them in getting the Congressional Committee position if they would tone down their proposals. Stop talking about confronting the Democrats, she said. Just promise to make sure the suffrage amendment is introduced in Congress, the one traditional job of the committee. A parade would also be a good idea, she thought.[16]

NAWSA's president, Anna Howard Shaw, without being overly enthusiastic, liked the idea of a parade. She had been to suffrage parades in London and New York. She had seen the passions they provoked and the support for suffrage they engendered. A parade in Washington might have the same effect.

With Addams's support, Paul and Burns tried again. This time they got what they were after. They were appointed to head NAWSA's Congressional Committee. They would have a budget of only ten dollars. The committee's sole responsibility, NAWSA reiterated, was to see that a constitutional amendment was introduced in the next session of Congress. But Paul and Burns were determined to go beyond that.

Awash in Suffrage News

As Paul made her way to Washington in December, the nation did not need to be made aware of the issue of suffrage. There was plenty of suffrage news:

- Suffrage amendments to state constitutions had been on the ballot in several states in November and had passed in three of them: Arizona, Oregon, and Kansas. They failed in Wisconsin and Ohio. Initial reports from Michigan had put the suffragists ahead, but subsequent counting had the suffragists losing by only about 6,000. Suffragists believed that vote fraud instigated by the liquor industry had cost them a victory.
- Maud Malone had achieved notoriety in October by challenging Democratic candidate Woodrow Wilson as he was delivering a campaign speech in Brooklyn. Dissatisfied with his answer that suffrage was not

Suffragist Maud Malone challenged Woodrow Wilson to take a stand on suffrage at one of his campaign appearances in October 1912. Dissatisfied with his answer, she continued to question him until she was forcibly removed from the building and arrested. (Library of Congress.)

something to be dealt with on a national level, Malone persisted in her questioning. She was then seized by police, taken out of the hall, and arrested. Three weeks later she was convicted of a misdemeanor. In late November she was still in the news, appealing her conviction.

- With the election results in, New York suffragists made a major push in the newly elected state legislature for an amendment to the state constitution. On November 9, a suffrage parade organized by Harriet Stanton Blatch drew 10,000 participants. There were nearly 400,000 onlookers as the parade made its way up Fifth Avenue. Blatch was the daughter of suffrage pioneer Elizabeth Cady Stanton and had lived in England for many years before returning to America. The suffrage parades she organized—this was not the first—arose from what she observed in Great Britain. The parades were peaceful and well executed.
- Socialite Rosalee Jones organized a group of "suffrage hikers" to walk from New York City to Albany in December in support of suffrage.
- Even the anti-suffragists were getting into the news. The New York State Association Opposed to Woman Suffrage issued a challenge to suffragists in November, saying it would not oppose a referendum on a New York constitutional amendment on suffrage during the next session of the legislature because it was sure the amendment would be defeated in a general election.

But the more exciting news was coming from across the Atlantic. News stories from London told of suffragists, frustrated at the lack of movement by the British government, carrying out guerilla tactics such as smashing windows, dropping open bottles of ink into mailboxes, spreading acid on golf courses, and threatening to do worse. They continually confronted politicians at public meetings and relished getting themselves hauled off by police. They introduced a word to the news media and the American public that sent many American suffragists scurrying: *militant.*

Some American suffragists—while certainly not adopting the label of militant—did not shy away from its meaning or some of its actions. Alice Paul was one of them.

Setting the Stage

When Paul arrived in Washington in mid-December (with Burns following soon after), she had hoped to build on what the previous Congressional Committees had done, particularly in compiling a list of local names she could call on. She found that the list was out of date and included mostly people who had died or had moved. She and Burns would have to create an organization from the ground up. That they did, in a marvel of social networking 1913-style.

Burns had already been in touch with Crystal Eastman Benedict, sister of radical journalist and editor Max Eastman and an old friend from her Vassar days. Crystal Eastman was living in Wisconsin with her husband, but her life and marriage were not what she had hoped, and she missed the vibrancy of the East Coast and her free-minded and feminist friends. Eastman headed east almost immediately.

Another call was made to Mary Beard, wife of historian Charles Beard. She had been active in suffrage and trade-union organizations in New York, where she had been part of the strike of shirtwaist factory workers in 1909. She too was eager to do something on the national stage.

Dora Lewis of Philadelphia, by far the oldest of the group, completed the first circle of parade planners. Paul and Lewis had become friends when they met during suffrage association meetings in Philadelphia, and despite their age difference, they shared similar attitudes about the direction the movement should take. Lewis's contacts with Philadelphia society would make her a valuable fund-raiser for the group.

Each of these women called, telegraphed, or wrote everyone she knew who would be interested in their idea: a suffrage parade down Pennsylvania Avenue in support of a federal amendment on the day before the inauguration of a new president. And they told those friends to contact their friends. It did not take long for word to spread and for volunteers to show up. Paul rented basement office space at 1420 F Street, only a couple of blocks from where the parade would take place, in the name of NAWSA's Congressional Committee. The office was in the middle of Washington's shopping district.

In late December, Paul had an official parade committee together and announced to journalists that there would be a suffrage parade on Pennsylvania Avenue on March 3. She did not yet have permission to use the avenue, nor did she have marchers or even a specific plan. But there was nothing tentative about the way journalists wrote about the parade. They absorbed it into stories about the coming inauguration, making it appear that it was a semi-official part of the inaugural ceremonies. Paul played on this connection by lining up prominent names, male and female, to associate with the parade. Suffrage had many friends in Washington, especially on Capitol Hill, and Paul exploited those friends to the fullest. In a December 29 *Washington Post* story about inaugural preparations, a subhead read: "Financial Chairman Thom Announces Fund Has Reached $35,125—Leaders Are Busy Choosing Assistants—Women Working Out Details for Big Suffrage Pageant on March 3—Large Party of Prominent Men Will Join Them."[17]

The suffragists were crashing the inaugural party, and there was little that inaugural planners could do about it.

All of this strengthened Paul's hand when, in early January, she approached District of Columbia officials about using Pennsylvania Avenue and obtaining police protection for the parade. She needed all of the advantages she could obtain because she was met with fierce opposition, particularly from Richard Sylvester, chief of police. Professing sympathy with the cause of suffrage, Sylvester suggested that Paul delay the parade until March 5, that she use another route, that his force wasn't big enough to protect the marchers, and that he didn't have the authority and wasn't inclined to ask for it. The U.S. Army was what she needed, he told her, not the D.C. police force.

He also said something Paul came to agree with. The march might be dangerous. The type of people likely to be on the street that day would not be inclined to respect the marchers or their cause. Sylvester said the November elections had been a Democratic victory, according to Paul's testimony before the Senate committee that later investigated the march:

> He said it was a Democratic victory, and the situation would be worse than it had been for years and years at inauguration time. This would mean that the riff-raff of the South would be here—those were his words—and it would be quite impossible for him to protect us; and he gave very alarming pictures of what Pennsylvania Avenue was at inauguration times.[18]

Paul had faced down London police, Holloway Prison, and force-feeding. She wasn't about to be dissuaded by District of Columbia officials or the possibility of "southern riff-raff" in the streets. She pressed for permission to use Pennsylvania Avenue on March 3. She called on friends to pull the congressional levers of power. The District was ruled directly by Congress, particularly by the committees with oversight in both the House and the Senate.

Paul exercised extraordinary leadership during these first weeks of the New Year by allowing others to carry the banner for various aspects of the parade. Although she was prominently mentioned in many of the news articles about preparations for the parade, those articles are filled with names of many other people who were chairing committees, engaging audiences, and raising money. From accounts of those who worked with her, there is no doubt that Paul was in charge; she would ask you to do something in a way that assumed your were going to do it; she also worked as hard as anyone, the first to be at the NAWSA offices in the morning and the last, along with Lucy Burns, to leave at night. But she never insisted on being the center of attention.

Paul kept her message simple. She wanted to have a parade. It wasn't fair that Sylvester and District officials would deny her and the women she represented that simple request. The *Washington Post* picked up on that theme on January 7 in an editorial supporting the suffragists:

> The American spirit of fair play demands that women be give the right to parade on Pennsylvania Avenue. If a parade on March 3 is desired by the women because it will give them great opportunity to attract attention to their propaganda, no obstacle should be placed in the way. They will not be molested. On the contrary, the visitors will watch the demonstration with interest and see in it, probably, the writing on the wall that will foretell the day when women everywhere will have the ballot.[19]

Permission came for the suffragists to use Pennsylvania Avenue two days later. But permission did not guarantee cooperation, especially from Chief of Police Sylvester, as Paul was to learn. Sylvester had made a number of public statements about how he didn't oppose the parade and that he was just trying to give the suffragists good advice. Many of the men on the force interpreted these statements as meaning they shouldn't go out of their way to help the suffragists. That message would eventually come back to haunt both Sylvester and the force.

Paul did not have time to reflect much on Sylvester's attitude. Details of the parade itself were overwhelming NAWSA's Washington office. Paul's idea of a parade had tapped a vast reserve of energy behind the idea of suffrage. Women from every part of the country said they were coming to Washington and promised to bring others with them.

Delegations were forming to supply floats, banners, and bands. A typical day in late January and February in the office was one of constant meetings, new ideas, activity, crises small and large, and decision-making. Paul was said to be so busy that she never had time to remove her hat.

Daily announcements about meetings, delegations coming from far-away states, plans for this person or that to be in the parade spewed forth from the F Street headquarters. There were even a few stunts, such as parade grand marshal Jane Burleson riding down F Street in full riding regalia on a horse. All of these generated the publicity that Paul was constantly seeking.

Publicity came from places other than the F Street office. In mid-January, New Yorker Rosalie Jones, fresh from leading a troop of suffrage hikers from New York City to Albany, announced she would be putting together another group to hike from New York to Washington for the parade. They would be carrying a special message to President Wilson to ask for his support for an amendment to the Constitution.[20] Journalists took up her stunt with good humor and always referred to her as "General" Jones and to themselves as "war correspondents."

One of the many decisions that Paul had to make was whether to allow a group of African American women from Howard University to march in the parade. Delegations of southern women had threatened to pull out of the parade if this happened, and Paul felt that she needed them more than she needed the Howard students. That attitude has been criticized by biographers and historians, but Paul (and other suffragists) was doing little more than reflecting the embedded racism of the times. Suffrage was a white, middle-class movement, and in that particular decade, it was not going to be anything else. The Howard University delegation ultimately was able to participate in the parade. It marched in the final section, and no mention was made of the delegation in the official program.

Through January and into February, suffrage speakers and meetings were constantly in the news. Some of these meetings were to be outdoors, which still generated interest from reporters. Inez Milholland, a favorite of journalists as

Alabama Representative Tom Heflin (*left*) became the target of suffragists as they planned for the parade, but his opposite number on the suffrage debate was Rep. Richmond Hobson (*right*), also from Alabama. Hobson openly supported suffrage and marched in the parade. He also was a vigorous champion of Prohibition and what became the Eighteenth Amendment. (Library of Congress.)

"the most beautiful suffragist," was announced on January 26 as the herald of the parade, an item that made page two of the *Washington Post* the next day.[21]

Suffrage news was also coming from across the Atlantic as Parliament, unsuccessfully, considered a suffrage measure for Great Britain. Through January there were regular reports of suffragists executing all manner of destruction (pouring acid on putting greens, throwing stones at the Tower of London) and threatening more (rumors of kidnapping Winston Churchill's infant, in one report) unless they got the franchise. Compared to them, a parade in Washington was pretty tame stuff.

Most American suffragists were determined not to travel down the road toward threats and violence. Still, even though they were getting plenty of attention from journalists, their daily announcements of meetings, endorsements, and parade plans were fairly bland. What they needed, and what the journalists covering them needed even more, were some sparks of opposition, conflict, and controversy. In the middle of February, a gentleman from the South stepped in to provide those sparks.

Alabama Representative Tom Heflin[22] had been invited to talk to a church group in Falls Church, Virginia, on the second Sunday in February. The *Washington Post* covered his speech, in which he was asked about the upcoming suffrage parade. Heflin didn't mince words. Women who participated in the march were working against the welfare of the nation, he said. "The cause of suffrage is a bad one. As has been said a million times, the place of a woman is at home, by the fireside, and in the bosom of her family."

The reporter lost no time in finding a suffragist to respond, one calling his remarks "Tommyrot." But Alice Paul's response was more measured, and more revealing. She welcomed his remarks: "Women do not vote in the East, yet there are thousands of women who are forced to work for a living and leave housework. The argument about the home sounds romantic and nice but it has no soundness to support it."[23]

Suffragists began mentioning Heflin in their talks and speeches, one calling him the "Beau Brummell of the House."[24] Another said he should be pitted in a debate with a prominent suffragist. All this gave journalists the excuse to ask him for a response, and he obliged. "My speech at Falls Church has been more or less twisted, for I did not attack them for the procession but for their action in chasing over Washington making speeches from automobiles. I think they could be doing much more at home."[25]

One suffragist suggested that parade herald Inez Milholland be paired in a debate with Heflin, a suggestion a *Washington Post* editorialist endorsed, tongue-in-cheek, saying a panel of impartial judges should declare a winner of

Inez Milholland was tagged by many journalists as "the most beautiful suffragist," but she was far more than a symbol. She was a forceful and dynamic speaker who, three days before the suffrage parade, learned that she had passed the New York bar exam. (Library of Congress.)

such an event. If it happened to be Milholland, women should immediately get the right to vote. "Or, if Mr. Heflin should win, then the women who are seeking the ballot would at once withdraw to their homes, and 'General' Rosalie Jones, having marched up the hill, could march right down again. What better way to settle the whole question."[26]

The Heflin-suffragist fandango was a journalistic contrivance but nonetheless revealed the way the journalism of the day worked and the skill that the suffragists showed in understanding and using it.

The suffragists were provided with a worthier and more substantive opponent when the National Association Opposed to Woman Suffrage showed up in Washington in mid-February. It announced the opening of an office and a giant anti-suffrage rally on Friday, February 28, three days before the parade. Though late to the game, the antis received substantial attention from journalists, sometimes with the same bemusement that they had given the suffragists. Once, after the antis' headquarters was opened on F Street just a block away from the NASWA headquarters, they complained that mud had been splattered on their windows and implied that it was the work of the suffragists or their sympathizers. When both organizations hired guards to watch over their headquarters at night, the *Washington Post* headlined the story: HELP, MEN, HELP![27]

The anti-suffragists took their arguments into the streets and to meetings just as the suffragists were doing. After a week of lobbying in Washington, Josephine Dodge, a New York activist who was president of the national association, claimed that Washington was an anti-suffragist city. "With the exception of the 40 representatives from the nine States that have equal suffrage, I could find few men in favor of votes for women."[28]

The large anti-suffrage meeting scheduled for the Friday afternoon before the suffrage parade on Monday was successful in that it was well attended and well covered by the press. Journalists noted that the Belasco Theater, in sight of the White House, was full to overflowing and the crowd included some noisy suffragists. But news accounts concentrated on what several of the speakers said and the arguments they made against suffrage. Endowing women with the right to vote could dilute the influence women have in society, cause damage to the home, and be of little benefit. Women working outside the home, according to one speaker, led to lessening the birthrate, lowering the "national vitality," and the general "deterioration of stock."[29]

The anti-suffrage rally on Friday was only part of a weekend full of the suffrage news, most of it concentrated on those coming to Washington to participate in the parade on Monday. A disproportionate amount of attention was given to the hikers from New York and their entry into the city on Friday when an enormous crowd of onlookers jammed the streets around their hotel. The failure of police to keep order then was an ominous sign as to what might happen on Monday. The suffragists held their own theater rally on Sunday evening and raised more than five thousand dollars to offset the parade expenses.

Throughout the weekend, meetings were held with Chief of Police Sylvester, who gave suffragists repeated assurances that all would be peaceful on Monday. But his answers and assurances were evasive enough to raise doubts. Paul asked Elizabeth Rogers, a sister-in-law to Secretary of War Henry Stimson, to approach Stimson about providing U.S. Army troops for security. Stimson's initial answer was that he could not legally do so. Still, he saw the potential dangers and sensed that the police might not be able to handle the crowds that would gather on Monday. He ordered the Fifteenth Cavalry from Ft. Myer, Virginia, to stay on the western side of Washington on Monday and be ready to move if called.

Bewildering Beauty

At some point after 3:15 p.m., Jane Burleson gave the signal for the parade to begin.[30] When she did, a trumpet herald was sounded, and she and her equestrian attendants began to move toward the Peace Monument and then left onto Pennsylvania Avenue. Inez Milholland followed a few yards behind them. On Burleson's left and right were flag-bearing aides on foot, walking slightly ahead of her. The women were spread out, assuming that they would have plenty of room to march.

Photographers snapped the shutters of their cameras to record the event.

For about four blocks along Pennsylvania Avenue, all went as planned, but when Burleson and Milholland reached Fifth Street, they had to stop. The people surrounding them were too numerous to proceed in an orderly fashion. Burleson described what she encountered as "this horrible howling mob, this jeering mob." She was fearful about what would happen to her and her attendants, she said. She also was fearful for Milholland and those behind her. The sixteen policemen who had accompanied her to that point had disappeared, she said, and she could find no evidence of them.[31]

Milholland's description put the same scene in a different light. Yes, she was surrounded, but she did not feel as though she was in any particular danger. She felt the crowd was generally good natured. Still, this wasn't what had happened to her when she was the herald for the Fifth Avenue suffrage parades in New York. She knew how these things were supposed to go, and this wasn't it.[32]

The suffragists had been assured of a cleared Pennsylvania Avenue no matter how big the crowd. Now, at three o'clock that afternoon, the avenue was not clear, and it was not going to be cleared. Getting up Pennsylvania Avenue during the next two hours would be a halting, frustrating, and sometimes scary struggle for Burleson, Milholland, and many of the rest of the parade participants for the remainder of the afternoon.

The crowds around Fourteenth Street and Pennsylvania Avenue had been growing since mid-morning. First scores, then hundreds, then thousands of people were packing themselves into the vicinity they believed would give them the best view of the parade and the pageant that was planned for the plaza in front of the Treasury building.

The pageant was an important part of the day's activities. A pageant, also called a tableau, was common in this pre-television age and could be elaborate, ornate, complex, and visually stunning.

Alice Paul believed that the pageant as much as the parade itself would establish the idea of equal rights for women—beginning with suffrage—in a pantheon of goals (such as liberty, freedom, justice) that all humans should strive for. The director of the pageant was Hazel MacKaye, well known as an artist, designer, and director.

The pageant was timed to start as the parade began at the other end of Pennsylvania Avenue. It would end as Burleson and Milholland rode by. The participants in the pageant would then stand in review as the parade passed by, fall in line behind it, and continue to Constitution Hall, where the last part of the pageant would be repeated.

The pageant did not start on time. The massive crowds around the Treasury building and back down Pennsylvania Avenue past Fourteenth Street made the streets impassable. The police that morning had stretched ropes at the curbs to try to keep the crowds off the street, but the ropes were easily defeated. People and traffic continued to pour into and through the Pennsylvania Avenue–Fourteenth Street area all morning and into the afternoon.

The parade itself was huge and stunning. Between 5,000 and 8,000 people, mostly women, participated as marchers, as horseback riders, or riders on floats. The order of the march had been meticulously planned to give the onlookers an interesting and arresting visual introduction to the idea of suffrage. A herald announced each section, and most sections featured women on horseback. The first section was devoted to the worldwide movement for suffrage and had delegations of women from countries that had achieved universal suffrage. A subsequent section featured delegations of professionals—women who were lawyers, farmers, teachers, doctors, and the like. Another section showed women in business, and yet another featured men who favored suffrage, particularly legislators. Sections included women from various states carrying signs showing their point of origin. The final section included Rosalie Jones and her suffrage pilgrims—a crowd favorite because of the publicity they had received during their hike to Washington.

Interspersed within the parade were colorful signs and banners. Paul had planned for the official colors of the parade to be white, purple, and green. NAWSA objected, saying that these were the colors of the English suffragists. The parade should emphasize the international suffrage colors of white and yellow, NAWSA officials said. A threat by

Anna Howard Shaw to withdraw from the parade forced Paul to back away from declaring white, purple, and green the official colors,[33] but they were still much in evidence during the parade.

Floats showing the history of women in America rolled by. Bands of various types provided music throughout the parade. Suffragists from Baltimore provided six "golden chariots" steered by prominent women of that city. One float titled "Women in the Fields" showed women with stalks of wheat and corn in their arms. Delegations of uniformed women representing teachers, writers, nurses, homemakers, artists, lawyers, ministers, and other disciplines marched with signs and banners. The *Washington Post* called the parade a "kaleidoscope of colors" and told its readers:

> Gay tunics set off somber caps and gowns; the prim dress of professional nurses were in the background for the gingham gowns and "poke" bonnets of the farming women, while the gay and fashionable attire of well-known actors was in contrast with the purposely ink-stained dresses of the literary women.[34]

At the lower end of Pennsylvania Avenue, those with an unobstructed or even a partial view would have been treated to a remarkable collection of people, signs, colors, and visual imagery that was dazzling. A viewer at the other end of the parade who could see both the parade and the pageant would have had a double visual treat. There the women and girls in front of the Treasury building had elaborate costumes or light, diaphanous gowns and moved in concert at the direction of the narrator. The city of Washington and most other cities in America had never seen anything like what Alice Paul had created that day. Even those spectators packed into the middle parts of the parade along Pennsylvania Avenue and distracted by the unruliness of the crowd had to have been impressed with the massive, coordinated spectacle they were witnessing.

The marchers were followed by people in automobiles that were draped with bunting and other regalia. The floats interspersed throughout the parade were elaborate and colorful, depicting the progress of women in American history. The parade was organized into seven sections, with each section having a theme.

Alice Paul had donned her academic robes for the parade, hoping to march with a group of Swarthmore graduates. When the head of the parade got into trouble with the crowd, she and Lucy Burns got into a car and drove slowly up the avenue, trying to move the crowds back to give the marchers room. Theirs was one of three cars challenging this ocean of humanity. The people on the edge of the marching path moved back slowly to avoid the oncoming cars. As soon as the cars had passed, they surged back into the street.

The police could do little, and in some cases did even less to help the marchers. The suffragists complained bitterly that the indifference of the police gave the crowd license to harass, intimidate, and assault the marchers, both verbally and physically. Janet Richards, one of the organizers of the march and a marshal in the first section of the parade, later spoke about the "spread of the mob spirit" among the crowd and attributed it to the breakdown of "police morale":

> From about 4 o'clock to 6 o'clock many of the police seemed to share in, and many of them to stimulate, the mob spirit. It was what they did not do that I saw. They seemed to give up. That is all. . . . [T]he tone and the inaction convinced me from that point on that the disposition to aid us had largely disappeared, at least with regard to the majority of the policemen.[35]

In some ways, the Woman Suffrage Procession was a victim of its own success. For the previous six weeks, news stories had continuously touted the marchers, the bands, the floats, and the general pageantry. There would be nothing like it in the foreseeable future. Even the inaugural parade would not compete, not if the words of its planners could be believed. They were emphasizing the dignity and simplicity of their event—descriptions not likely to attract a huge crowd. (The inaugural planners had sought some political advantage in stressing the event's simplicity. "Jeffersonian simplicity and dignity, in the real meaning of the term, will mark the inauguration of President-elect Wilson," the *Washington Post* reported on December 26. An "inaugural carnival" would not be held, according to the *New York Times* on December 27, because it would detract from the dignity of the occasion.)

Photographs taken from several stories above the Fourteenth Street area that afternoon after the parade had begun show a solid mass of people. Getting the street clear at that point was probably more than the police and their deputized assistants could manage even if they had tried. In many places, there were simply too many people and not enough room to push people back onto the curbs.

Burleson should have needed only about forty-five minutes to lead the parade up Pennsylvania Avenue to the plaza of the Treasury building. It took more than twice that long. (The members of the pageant at the Treasury building were supposed to watch the parade as soon as they completed the pageant. They finished well before the parade was over and stood there for as long as they could stand it—many were bare-footed because of the dancing and movements the pageant required. Finally they had to retreat inside the building to wait for more than an hour.) Along the way, parade participants encountered three inter-linking problems: the lack of space, the crowd, and the unwillingness or inability of the police to assist them.[36]

Lack of Space

Without question, Pennsylvania Avenue was not the cleared path that it should have been on the afternoon of March 3, 1913—and not the clear path that it would be on March 4 when the new president and the inaugural parade would take the same route. There were simply too many people in the space between Fourth Street and the Treasury building past Fifteenth Street for the avenue to be free of onlookers.

Once the parade began, district officials tried to clear a path for the marchers by driving cars slowly in front of the parade. At some points where the crowd had thinned out a bit, this worked. But in many cases it did not. As soon as the cars passed, the crowd simply closed—the word used by marchers was "surged"—back into the space left in the cars' wake. The crowds were so thick and the marchers' lane so small that, on numerous occasions, a line that was supposed to be five or six abreast would be reduced to one person.

The District officials who were trying to handle the situation became so frustrated that they notified the War Department and asked for the help of the U.S. Cavalry. The horseback troops responded and, coming from the west, met Burleson at about Fourteenth Street. They rode back down Pennsylvania Avenue, attempting to get people to move back. As the trained horsemen maneuvered their mounts back and forth, they were more successful than the cars in pushing the onlookers back and clearing a wider lane for the marchers. The latter sections of the parade were able to march without the interference that the first part had to endure.

Still, there was a cost. Large numbers of people in small spaces do not move in concert, and there was much pushing, shoving, stumbling, and general chaos—although the way the troops worked, that chaos was probably localized. What the troops did must have resulted in some injuries and confusion and must have created some fear and anger among the onlookers. Without attributing injuries to what the Army troops did, the *Washington Post* described their actions:

> The men in brown virtually brushed aside the mounted and foot police and took charge. In two lines the troop [*sic*] charged the crowds. Evidently realizing they would be ridden down, the people fought their way back. When they

hesitated, the cavalrymen, under orders of their officers, did not hesitate. Their horses were driven into the throngs and whirled and wheeled until hooting men and women were forced to retreat. A space was quickly cleared.[37]

The Crowd

Was the crowd a "howling mob," as Jane Burleson said, or one that was reasonably good natured? The answer is probably "both."

The people watching the parade were not the respectful group—applauding and cheering as the floats, bands, and delegations passed by—that the suffragists had hoped for. They were also not the nefarious band of ruffians that some suffragists later claimed. Undoubtedly, there were those who were drunk and disrespectful and did not pay attention to the order of the parade. Some called the marchers names and said uncouth things that white, middle-class women normally do not hear. Sensing the freedom that comes from a lack of visible authority, some people acted out.

Senator Albert Johnson of Washington (a suffrage state) told the Senate committee investigating the parade that he observed the parade from a second-floor restaurant near Fourteenth Street. He described a man, "a mischief maker," who was selling notions and kept talking in a very loud voice all afternoon:

> He would call out. The first part of the parade was a young lady on horseback, and as I told you the people where I sat were strangers. They did not know any of the prominent persons, so this fellow called out, "Three cheers for Gen. Jones." Everybody in my vicinity began to think that this must be Gen. Jones. I heard them talking back and forth, and finally they got it straightened out that this was not Gen. Jones. Then a little bit later the parade came along, and he called out in a loud voice—he was a street faker and he had one of those loud voices. He called out, "There is Carrie Nation." And of course that started everyone in my vicinity looking for Carrie Nation. Finally someone explained that she was dead and had been dead for a long time, and that started a hubbub.[38]

But there were also acts of violence about which the marchers properly complained. Some of the marchers and participants on the floats were grabbed and harassed. Banners and signs were torn out of their hands. Some of the suffragists reported being spat upon and having lighted matches and cigarettes tossed into their ranks. The male marchers were tagged by loudmouths throughout the route as "Henpecko," and some of the women endured various examples of "barnyard language."

Occasionally, the women fought back. Dr. Nellie Mark of Baltimore told the Senate committee that, as she was marching with the professional women of Maryland, she carried a baton and did not hesitate to use it on those who interfered with her or her comrades. At one point, someone in the crowd grabbed a young woman in front of her, and Dr. Mark came to her rescue. "I hit him crack on the nose, and I am positive his nose is swollen to this day." She also told of sticking her baton into the mouth of another rowdy and being certain that she heard him swallow some teeth. A senator asked if she hit anyone else. "No, I was waiting, but they seemed to keep back."[39]

The *Washington Post* on the day after the parade reported about one hundred people being hurt or needing medical assistance.[40] It was not clear how many of these people were marchers and how many were members of the crowd. Other estimates of those injured were higher, but no one was reported seriously injured. The intoxicated and unruly men, the altercations, and the injuries melded into what became the overall narrative of the suffrage parade.

The Police

As with the crowd, the record of the District of Columbia police in handling the Washington suffrage parade is mixed. On the ground, some policemen tried their best to do what they could to give the marchers room to parade up Pennsylvania Avenue. Many of those who testified before the Senate committee or filed affidavits said that, from their points of view, the policemen were doing their duty.

But many other policemen did not, and the suffragists (and others) were not timid about telling those stories:

DR. NELLIE MARK: "Another case in which I did call the attention of the police to it [interference of the crowd] was that a young lady in the brigade in front of mine, who was grabbed and chucked under the chin, and the man tried to put his arm around her. I called to the policeman. He paid no attention. He looked and smiled and seemed to enjoy it. I rushed to the rescue of the girl because her clothes were being torn."[41]

H. ANNA QUINBY: "[T]here were an abundance of policemen along the line of the march, but not one of them made any attempt to keep the people back . . . and on one occasion a policeman talked saucy to an elderly woman who asked him to make the crowd stand back."[42]

ABBY SCOTT BAKER: "They were standing with arms folded and they were laughing with the crowd. The crowd was calling out stupid things, you know, and the policemen looked amused, and some I saw standing talking to the crowd with their backs to the marchers. Sometimes they would wave, what do you call the—their sticks, a little. But most of them were not doing anything at all."[43]

Numerous other witnesses said they saw policemen not only failing to protect the suffragists but making rude and insulting remarks. That the police did this and were so open about it leads to the conclusion that they felt safe in doing so. It was undoubtedly known through the department that Major Sylvester did not like the idea of a parade and had tried to persuade the suffragists not to hold it. One argument he made was that he did not have enough men to properly staff it. While he wrote and promulgated elaborate plans for security for the parade, many of the men on the force did not take them seriously enough to try to prevent anything untoward from happening.

Further evidence of this attitude came to light when Walter Thiesen, a staff photographer for the *Philadelphia Evening Times,* came to Washington on Sunday and stopped by the police department seeking credentials for shooting

The Washington Post.

Weather—Fair this morning; cloudy in afternoon and unsettled and somewhat colder at night. Temperature yesterday—Maximum, 39; minimum, 23.

NO. 13,417. WASHINGTON: TUESDAY, MARCH 4, 1913.—TWENTY-SIX PAGES. TWO CENTS.

WOMAN'S BEAUTY, GRACE, AND ART BEWILDER THE CAPITAL

Miles of Fluttering Femininity Present Entrancing Suffrage Appeal.

PAGEANT, LIVING PICTURES, ORATORY

Richly Decorated Floats Tell the History and Point to the Future of Equal Rights Struggle — Entrancing Spectacle at Times Is Marred by Scenes of Disorder Along the Line of March — Procession, Blocked by Throngs, Moves Only Ten Blocks in an Hour — United States Troops From Fort Myer Come to Rescue. "General" Jones, Leading Her Pilgrims on Foot, Is Popular Heroine.

Five thousand women, marching in the woman suffrage pageant yesterday, practically fought their way foot by foot up Pennsylvania avenue, through a surging mass of humanity that completely defied the Washington police, swamped the marchers, and broke their procession into little companies. The women, trudging stoutly along under great difficulties, were able to complete their march only when troops of cavalry from Fort Myer were rushed into Washington to take charge of Pennsylvania avenue. No inauguration has ever produced such scenes, which in many instances amounted to little less than riots.

Criticise Police Inactivity.

Later, in Continental Hall, the women turned what was to have been a suffrage demonstration into an indignation meeting, in which the Washington police were roundly criticised for their inactivity. an dresolutions were passed calling upon President-elect Wilson and the incoming Congress to make an investigation and locate the responsibility for the indignities the marchers suffered. Miss Helen Keller, the noted deaf and blind girl, was so exhausted and unnerved by the experience in attempting to reach a grand stand

STRIKING TABLEAUX BY SUFFRAGETTES.

Photo by Harris & Ewing.

100 ARE IN HOSPITAL

Crowds Trample Men; Women Faint in the Crush.

BLOCK WORK OF SURGEONS

SICK DRIVEN AWAY

Police Rough With Sufferers Seeking Dr. Friedmann.

THOUSANDS DESIRE CURE

Men and Women Weep When Doctor

WOODROW WILSON ARRIVES TO BECOME NATION'S HEAD TODAY

PRESIDENT AND VICE PRESIDENT TODAY.

WOODROW WILSON. THOMAS R. MARSHALL.
Photo © Harris Ewing.

Democracy to the Number of 250,000 Comes to Inaugurate President.

STATE EXECUTIVES AND SOLDIERY HERE

Future Cabinet Officers Are Given Ovations as They Pass—Taft Rides Through Vast Throng Here to Celebrate Victory of His Successor—Seven Trains Unload Tammany "Braves" for Carnival—Officials of Ceremonies Find Time Only for Completing Arrangements. Retire Happy Because Weather Forecaster Says Day Will Be Fair—Epoch-making Event Will Commence at Noon, When Marshall Is Sworn In.

Woodrow Wilson, of New Jersey, has come to Washington to be inaugurated today the twenty-seventh President of the United States.

His was a triumphal entry, the pent-up Democratic enthusiasm of sixteen years concentrating seemingly at the gateway of the Nation's Capital and bursting forth in a joyful acclaim.

Preceding the next President of the United States came other distinguished visitors, governors, cabinet possibilities, and world celebrities. Every train poured a fresh mass of humanity into the city, until it was estimated that 250,000 strangers were here.

Bryan Hailed as "Mr. Secretary."

William Jennings Bryan was one of the early arrivals. He came as a "plain citizen," he said, but soon he was being addressed as "Mr. Secretary."

Mr. Bryan greeted hundreds of Democrats from all sections of the country in an informal reception when he reached his hotel.

While the President-elect under the same roof in an upper room was shaking hands with his old college chums from Princeton, the future Secretary of State also was the recipient of countless con-

'WELCOME, WILSON'

Cohorts Cheer President-Elect From Station to Hotel.

OFFICIAL GUEST OF CITY

CABINET LIST READY

Wilson Will Send Names to Senate This Afternoon.

TWO COME AS SURPRISES

The *Washington Post* front page the day after the suffrage parade showed how successful Alice Paul had been in capturing the attention of Washington, the capital's journalists, and the nation as a whole. (Courtesy of the *Washington Post*.)

MANY CALL MONDAY'S OUTRAGE BLOT ON FAIR NAME OF CAPITAL

Leaders in Suffragist Protest Against Inefficient Police Protection

At Top, Left to Right—MISS ALICE PAUL and MRS. HELEN H. GARDENER Taking Testimony at Suffrage Headquarters—Photo by G. V. Buck.

Single Picture at Right—MRS. ROBERT BAKER.—Photo by Harris & Ewing.

Group Picture at Bottom; Left to Right; First Row—MISS DORRIS C. STEVENS, Dayton, Ohio; MRS. JAMES A. MARLAY, Dayton, Ohio; MRS. GLENNA S. TINNIN, Washington, D. C.; MRS. KEPPELE HALL, Dayton, Ohio; daughter of Malcome Hay, Pittsburg, Pa. Back Row—MRS. M. A. WOOD, MISS ALICE VIGNOS, Canton, Ohio; MISS HARDEN, MRS. S. M. COLEMAN, daughter of General Moseby; MISS BLANCHE VIGNOS, Canton, Ohio, daughter of Major Vignos, Member State Board for Investigating Women's Work in Ohio.
—Photo by G. V. Buck

North Carolina Naval Reserves Are Rescued

Two Men Are Injured When Scaffold Falls

Warner's Safe Remedies

Health and the Kidneys

CLEARANCE SALE

Women's Up-to-the-Minute Sample Shoes, in the Latest Dressy Models, and All Leathers.

$1⁹⁵

$3.50 to $7.00 Values

SAMPLE SHOES

For Men, Women and Boys

Men's High Grade Sample Shoes in all the Newest Styles and Leathers

$2⁴⁵

$3.50

Let Postum Cheer This Lucky Year

Headlines generated by the U.S. Senate committee's investigation of what happened at the suffrage parade helped construct the narrative about the parade. Suffragists took full advantage of the impressions formed by journalists and the public of what had happened. (Courtesy of the *Washington Times*.)

the parade the next day and for shooting the inaugural parade on Tuesday. According to the affidavit he filed with the Senate committee, he was told, "You will need a pass for the inaugural procession but will not need one for the damn suffragettes." Then, on Monday, he was ordered off Pennsylvania Avenue by a policeman who said, "You ought to be ashamed to give them space in your paper."[44]

The parade finally ended early that evening, and many of the marchers gathered in Continental Hall (now known as Constitution Hall). Despite the problems many of the participants encountered, there was a generally upbeat note to the final parts of the procession, mainly due to the presence of "General" Rosalie Jones and her hikers. They had received a lion's share of the late February pre-parade publicity, and they drew loud cheers all along Pennsylvania Avenue. Many of the onlookers had turned out just to see them.

The Continental Hall gathering, rather than being a celebration of the parade and a presentation of the arguments in favor of suffrage, turned into an "indignation" meeting. NAWSA president Anna Howard Shaw excoriated the capital city: "Never was I so ashamed of our national capital before." Calls were made to condemn the conduct of the Washington police and for Congress to conduct an investigation.

Privately, the suffrage leaders were delighted with what had happened. The parade had been conducted with much dignity and grace, they felt, and the problems that occurred could not be laid at the feet of the women. The suffragists had captured half of the *Washington Post*'s front page the next day under the laudatory headline: "WOMAN'S BEAUTY, GRACE, AND ART BEWILDER THE CAPITAL"[45]

More significantly, the women had picked up a new enemy in their quest for suffrage to become a serious political issue: the Washington police force. In the coming days, they would exploit that enemy for all its worth.

Hearings and Headlines

Suffragist friends in Congress—and those concerned with running the District of Columbia—wasted no time in forming a committee to look into what happened during the suffrage parade. Three days after the parade, an inquiry was convened, and testimony was taken. The hearings continued for most of the next two weeks and generated plenty of headlines, along with a storyline that favored suffragists and the idea of votes for women. The committee adjourned for the rest of March but resumed meeting for a few days in April. Its final report was issued on May 29.

One of the star witnesses was the chief of police himself. Richard Sylvester offered a variety of reasons why things had not gone well with the parade. He complained that he did not have enough men to maintain order in such a large crowd. He said Congress had not given him the authority to clear the street in time for that to happen. His plans for the day, which he submitted with his testimony, were detailed and comprehensive. His officers, he said, did not follow his orders. "The failure of the police to protect was contrary to discipline, contrary to law, contrary to justice, contrary to my express orders, and the man who failed to do his part toward protecting these women should be immediately dismissed."[46]

Sylvester had not been present at the beginning of the parade. He went to Union Station as part of the escort for President-elect Wilson, who arrived during the parade. Sylvester, when he returned from escorting Wilson to his hotel, said he was "shocked and surprised" to see Pennsylvania Avenue overflowing with people.

Sylvester's testimony confirmed the obvious—that the suffragists had been subjected to conditions and abuse that would not have happened had the police done their job properly. What Sylvester said also added credence to the many stories that suffragists told the committee about police neglect, apathy, intransigence, and even interference.

A devastating contrast emerged from the suffragists' testimony. Troops of Boy Scouts had been recruited to help usher the marchers down the avenue, and many of them wound up trying to keep the crowd at bay. Several people

The 1913 Washington Suffrage Parade

testified that they saw the scouts working hard at this task while policemen simply stood and watched. One of the scouts, twelve-year-old Phillip Elliott, testified to the committee that, while he was trying to help, a policeman pushed him down:

> I was trying to help keep the crowds back, and this policeman did not want me to interfere. He was pushing the people back. He sort of caught me by the side of the head and pushed me down, and I have a little bump on the top of my head. It did not matter much of anything; but, as mother said, she thought it was quite a brutal act on the part of the policeman.[47]

Headlines generated by these hearings told the story of orderly, dignified women in sight of the U.S. Capitol building facing an unruly crowd that was ignored or even aided by the police:

POLICE MUST EXPLAIN; Senate Takes Up Suffrage Case and Orders Inquiry.

(*Washington Post,* March 6, p. 1)

POLICE IDLY WATCHED ABUSE OF WOMEN; Shocking Insults to Suffrage Paraders Testified To at Washington Inquiry. EVEN SEIZED AND SPAT UPON Girl on a Float Tells How She Kicked in the Face a Man Who Grasped Her Ankle.

(*New York Times,* March 7, p. 1)

SAY POLICE URGED MOB ON IN INSULTS TO WOMEN HIKERS; Leading Suffragists Tell Senate Committee of Affronts Given Them During Parade. WHITE GUARDS JOIN JEERS Officer Tears Dress of Marcher When She Hits Man Who Spit Tobacco in Friend's Face. FLOAT GIRLS USE FEET AS WEAPONS

(*Chicago Daily Tribune,* March 7, p. 1)

SYLVESTER SHOCKED AT INSULTS TO WOMEN; Washington Police Chief Puts Blame for Suffrage Parade Disorder on Officers and Men. **FAVORS INSTANT DISMISSAL** Stimson Says at Senate Inquiry That He Stretched the Law in Ordering the Troop of Cavalry.

(*New York Times,* March 9, p. 23)

SUFFRAGE ARMY LEADERS PROTEST; Tell of Poor Police Protection on March 3d Before the Senate Committee **ARMY CHIEFS CRITICISED** Major Sylvester Says Huge Inaugural Crowds Could Not Be Kept Off Avenue

(*San Francisco Chronicle,* March 9, p. 53)

CENSURE POLICE OF WASHINGTON; Four Senators Denounce Inadequate Protection of the Suffrage Parade. **TALK AT MASS MEETING.** Arguments Made in Favor of Allowing Women a Voice in the Government.

(*Chicago Daily Tribune,* March 10, p. 6)

The final report of the committee criticized but exonerated Sylvester for the most part and found that the police had been indifferent to providing the parade with adequate protection. Still, the report said, the actions of a few officers should not reflect on the character of the department as a whole. Suffragists and editorialists alike were dissatisfied with the committee's conclusions and thereafter often used the term "whitewash" to describe them.

Suffragists took full advantage of these developments and at every opportunity tied the unruly mob and the actions of the police to those who opposed votes for women. The conduct of the crowd, wrote Alice Stone Blackwell, editor of *Woman's Journal,* with its "ugliness and stupidity" was akin to the actions and attitudes of anti-suffragists.[48] Undoubtedly, the events of March 1913 put the anti-suffragists on the defensive. Some believed that what happened on Pennsylvania Avenue on the afternoon of March 3 converted people indifferent or opposed to suffrage into proponents.

The parade, said Congressman Clyde Tavenner, resulted in more votes for suffrage "than will perhaps ever be made again in the same length of time so long as the government stands."[49]

The Washington suffrage parade and its aftermath resulted in some attitude adjustment among American journalists and editors. In a study of editorial reaction to the parade, Linda Lumkin found the "uniformly outraged tone of editorials show that the press acknowledged women have civil rights" and such an acknowledgment was one step away from support for women's right to vote.[50]

But suffrage still had a tortuous political road to travel. It would be seven and a half years before the Tennessee legislature on a hot August day in Nashville became the thirty-sixth state to ratify the Nineteenth Amendment, thereby making it a part of the U.S. Constitution. Alice Paul and Lucy Burns would split from the NAWSA completely and form a new political party—one that would pioneer a new form of protest by picketing the White House. NAWSA itself would change leadership and shift its focus from state-by-state campaigns to obtaining a constitutional amendment. A world war and a politically fractured peace would intervene.

What was evident in the spring of 1913 was that, aided by the Washington parade, the idea of women's suffrage had gone beyond the "stage of ridicule" that Alice Paul had identified only three years earlier. The nation had very literally seen suffrage and would now have to deal with it—and ultimately accept it.

Notes

1. U.S. Senate, *Suffrage Parade: Hearings before a subcommittee of the Committee on the District of Columbia, part 1,* March 4–17, 1913, 494–95, http://books.google.com/books?id=YsEAAAAYAAJ&printsec=frontcover#v=onepage&q=Jeanette%20Richards&f=false (hereafter *Suffrage Parade*

2. Linda J. Lumsden, *Inez: The Life and Times of Inez Milholland* (Bloomington: Indiana University Press, 2004), 84.

3. See Mary Walton, *A Woman's Crusade: Alice Paul and the Battle for the Ballot* (New York: Palgrave Macmillan, 2010), and Christine Lunardini, *From Equal Suffrage to Equal Rights: Alice Paul and the National Woman's Party, 1912–1928* (New York: New York University Press, 1986).

4. "Taft Is Hissed by Suffragists," *Washington Post,* April 15, 1910, http://proxy.lib.utk.edu/docview/145013796?accountid=14766.

5. See John Milton Cooper, *Pivotal Decades: The United States, 1900–1920* (New York: W. W. Norton, 1990), and Jackson Lears, *Rebirth of a Nation: The Making of Modern America, 1877–1920* (New York: HarperCollins, 2009).

6. Richard Kielbowicz, "The Media and Reform, 1900–1917," in William David Sloan, James G. Stovall, and James D. Startt, eds., *The Media in America: A History* (2nd ed., Scottsdale, AZ: Publishing Horizons, 1993), 330.

7. Frank Luther Mott, *American Journalism: A History: 1690–1962* (New York: Macmillan, 1962), 503, quoting the *Nation* 56 (April 27, 1893): 306.

8. See Mitchell Stephens, *A History of News: From the Drum to the Satellite* (New York: Viking, 1988).

9. Michael Carleback, *American Photojournalism Comes of Age* (Washington, DC: Smithsonian Institution Press, 1997), 2.

10. Many photographs from the achieves of these services now reside in the Library of Congress. Photos from those three services make up the bulk of the pictures in this book.

11. Mary E. Cookingham, "Bluestockings, Spinsters and Pedagogues: Women College Graduates, 1865–1910," *Population Studies* 38, no. 3 (November 1984): 349–64. Published by Population Investigation Committee, http://www.jstor.org/stable/2174128.

12. The fact that a woman had a job and supported herself did not automatically make her a suffragist. Suffragists were a small minority even among women. Female anti-suffragists were prominent in every walk of life. This was particularly true of some prominent female journalists. See Amber Roessner and Jim Stovall, "Another Side of Woman's Suffrage: The Journalistic Stances of Sarah Hale, Jane Cunningham Croly, and Ida Tarbell," paper presented to the Symposium on the Nineteenth Century Press, the Civil War, and Free Expression, University of Tennessee–Chattanooga, November 11, 2011.

13. "Won't Try to Start Suffrage War Here," *New York Times*, January 2, 1910, http://proxy.lib.utk.edu/docview/97053237?accountid=14766.

14. The parade in which Paul participated was the third of its kind, the first being held in 1907. Each of these events involved thousands of marchers and many more onlookers. See Lisa Tickner, *The Spectacle of Women: Imagery of the Suffrage Campaign, 1907–1914* (Chicago: University of Chicago Press, 1988).

15. Lunardini, *From Equal Suffrage to Equal Rights,* 5–9. Other American suffragists influenced by Pankhurst included Inez Haynes Irwin, Harriot Stanton Blatch, Nora Blatch (Harriot's daughter), Mary Ritter Beard, Alva Belmont, and Elizabeth Robins.

16. Lunardini, *From Equal Suffrage to Equal Rights,* 21.

17. "Eustis Selects 135," *Washington Post,* December 29, 1912, http://proxy.lib.utk.edu/docview/145156714?accountid=14766.

18. *Suffrage Parade Hearings,* 132.

19. "The Suffrage Parade," *Washington Post,* January 7, 1913, http://proxy.lib.utk.edu/docview/145202408?accountid=14766.

20. "Motive for Pageant," *Washington Post,* January 13, 1913, http://proxy.lib.utk.edu/docview/145219646?accountid=14766. The disposition of that message would later cause some controversy when NAWSA's leadership announced that they, not the hikers, would meet with Wilson. The hikers took offense and let their feelings be know. NAWSA quickly backed off and made peace with the hikers.

21. "Will Ride as Heralds," *Washington Post,* January 27, 1913, http://proxy.lib.utk.edu/docview/145235508?accountid=14766.

22. James Thomas Heflin was already well known in Washington by 1913. In 1908 he had confronted a black man on a streetcar and shot and seriously wounded him. He was indicted, but charges were later dropped. In 1920 he was elected to the U.S. Senate but failed to get the Democratic nomination for Senate after he supported Herbert Hoover in 1928. His final Senate speech was a five-hour diatribe filled with gestures and racial jokes.

23. "Challenge to Heflin," *Washington Post,* February 13, 1913, http://proxy.lib.utk.edu/docview/145237648?accountid=14766.

24. "Suffragists Call Mr. Heflin Beau Brummell of the House," *Washington Post,* February 12, 1913, http://proxy.lib.utk.edu/docview/145221808?accountid=14766. Beau Brummell was a nineteenth-century British dandy, famous for his clothes and vapid lifestyle.

25. "Heflin Only Amused," *Washington Post,* February 14, 1913, http://proxy.lib.utk.edu/docview/145231771?accountid=14766.

26. "Milholland-Heflin Debate," *Washington Post,* February 17, 1913, http://proxy.lib.utk.edu/docview/145231637?accountid=14766.

27. "Mice Scatter Army," *Washington Post,* February 21, 1913, http://proxy.lib.utk.edu/docview/145260963?accountid=14766.

28. "Anti Claims Capital," *Washington Post,* February 26, 1913, http://proxy.lib.utk.edu/docview/145192712?accountid=14766.

29. "Jam Anti Meeting," *Washington Post,* March 1, 1913, http://proxy.lib.utk.edu/docview/145236409?accountid=14766. Lisa Tickner argues effectively that forcing the anti-suffragists into an organization and making them articulate their argument ultimately helped the suffragists in England (and, by extension, in America). "Once anti-suffragist opinion was organised publicly it was obliged to mobilise residual prejudice into rational argument, and in doing so it helped to clear away apathy and indifference, which in the suffragists' view was the most serious obstacle to their own campaign" (Tickner, *The Spectacle of Women,* 99).

30. It is not clear whether she received a signal from the pageant directors or simply started the parade on her own.

31. *Suffrage Parade Hearings,* 496.

32. Lumsden, *Inez,* 84–86.

33. Sidney R. Bland, "New Life in an Old Movement: Alice Paul and the Great Suffrage Parade of 1913 in Washington, D.C.," *Records of the Columbia Historical Society, Washington, D.C.* 71–72 (1971–72): 657–78.

34. "Woman's Beauty, Grace, and Art Bewilder the Capital," *Washington Post,* March 4, 1913, http://proxy.lib.utk.edu/docview/145222197?accountid=14766.

35. *Suffrage Parade Hearings,* 177.

36. For additional descriptions and analysis of the parade, see Lunardini, *From Equal Suffrage to Equal Rights,* 27–30; Walton, *A Woman's Crusade,* 72–80; and Katherine H. Adams and Michael L. Keene, *Alice Paul and the American Suffrage Campaign* (Urbana: University of Illinois Press, 2008), 79–92. An article that concentrates on the pageant is S. J. Moore, "Making a Spectacle of Suffrage: The National Woman Suffrage Pageant, 1913," *Journal of American Culture* 20 (1997): 89–103.

37. "Woman's Beauty, Grace, and Art Bewilder the Capital."

38. *Suffrage Parade Hearings,* 423–24.

39. *Suffrage Parade Hearings,* 475.

40. "Woman's Beauty, Grace, and Art Bewilder the Capital."

41. *Suffrage Parade Hearings,* 478.

42. *Suffrage Parade Hearings,* 509.

43. *Suffrage Parade Hearings,* 35.

44. *Suffrage Parade Hearings,* 459.

45. "Woman's Beauty, Grace, and Art Bewilder the Capital."

46. "Sylvester Shocked at Insults to Women," *New York Times,* March 9, 1913, http://proxy.lib.utk.edu/docview/97442191?accountid=14766.

47. *Suffrage Parade Hearings,* 74.

48. Quoted in Bland, "New Life in an Old Movement," 675.

49. Quoted in Bland, "New Life in an Old Movement," 676.

50. Linda J. Lumsden, "Beauty and the Beasts: Significance of Press Coverage of the 1913 National Suffrage Parade," *Journalism and Mass Communication Quarterly* 77, no. 3 (Autumn 2000): 602.

The Photographs

Planning the Parade

Plans for a gigantic suffrage parade along Pennsylvania Avenue in Washington, D.C., began as soon as Alice Paul and Lucy Burns convinced the National American Woman Suffrage Association to put them in charge of its Congressional Committee in late November 1912. Paul and Burns set about immediately contacting friends and anyone sympathetic to the idea. If they were going to pull this off on the day they intended—March 3, 1913, the day before Woodrow Wilson was to be inaugurated president—they had only three months.

PHOTOGRAPH 1: Alice Paul, shown here, appropriately, in academic robes, was the instigator and moving force behind the parade. She put together the people and made all of the major decisions about the timing and makeup of the parade. Paul was a Quaker from New Jersey who graduated from Swarthmore College in 1905. She exemplified a new type of woman who was entering the suffrage movement—young, well-educated, and impatient with the internal quarrels and state-by-state strategy of the National American Woman Suffrage Association (NAWSA). Paul believed that strategy should be abandoned for a national push that would gain a suffrage amendment to the U.S. Constitution. Her first step in doing that would be to stage the first national suffrage parade. The pin she is wearing on the front of her graduation hood is the Holloway broach, earned for her time as a suffragist in Holloway Prison in England. Paul would later produce an American version of this pin for those suffragists who had been jailed for picketing the White House.

PHOTOGRAPH 2: Lucy Burns met Alice Paul in London, where they were both detained after a suffrage demonstration. Burns shared Paul's zeal and intensity for gaining suffrage. Although the opposite of Paul in many ways—she was a tall, red-headed Catholic from Brooklyn with a vivacious personality—she and Paul seemed to work perfectly together. Burns had a degree from Vassar, which gave her many contacts to call upon while planning the parade.

The Photographs

PHOTOGRAPH 3: Mary Beard was one of the first people that Burns and Paul called on when they began planning the parade. Beard was a member of the Women's Trade Union League and one of the organizers of the 1909 shirtwaist makers' strike in New York City. She was the wife of influential historian Charles Beard, and she understood the workings of how to organize many people for one purpose.

PHOTOGRAPH 4: Crystal Eastman had been a classmate of Burns's at Vassar and was a committed proponent of suffrage. She had a master's degree from Columbia University and a law degree from New York University. Her brother, Max Eastman, was the editor of *The New Masses,* a radical political and literary journal. Eastman had married an insurance agent, Wallace Benedict, and had moved with him to Wisconsin. By late 1912, she knew the marriage was not working as she had hoped, and she missed the vibrancy of her radical circles on the East Coast. When Burns called on her to help, she did not hesitate.

PHOTOGRAPH 5: Dora Lewis and Alice Paul met after Paul had returned from England in 1910 and enrolled at the University of Pennsylvania in Philadelphia. Paul began attending meetings of the local suffrage association and found that Lewis, despite being much older than Paul, shared the dissatisfaction and impatience that Paul had with the lack of progress that NAWSA had made on gaining the vote for women. Lewis knew many people inside Philadelphia's Main Line social circles, and Paul knew she would be a valuable presence for many reasons, including fundraising. Eventually Lewis would follow Paul out of NAWSA and into the National Woman's Party, where she would be arrested for picketing the White House. The hunger strike and force-feeding she endured while in jail would nearly kill her.

PHOTOGRAPH 6 (*facing page*): Even before Paul and Burns had fully settled in Washington, Paul had put together a committee of women and given them assignments. In addition to Dora Lewis, Crystal Eastman, and Mary Beard, this committee took major responsibilities for making the parade happen. They are (*seated, left to right*) Glenna Tinnin, organizer of the pageant; Helen Gardner, the chief press agent for the committee; Alice Paul; Elizabeth Kent, chair of the bands committee and organizer of the post-parade meeting at Continental Hall; Genevieve Stone, wife of Illinois Congressman Claude Stone and chair of the marching delegations from non-suffrage states; (*standing, left to right*) Gertrude Leonard, a lawyer who was in charge of the Washington suffrage headquarters; Nina Allender, an artist and organizer of the outdoor meetings that advertised the parade; an unidentified woman, possibly Lulu Hemingway, chair of the committee that put together much of the literature that advertised the parade; Hazel MacKaye, a noted artist and director who directed the pageant on the plaza of the U.S. Treasury building during the parade; and Elsie Hill, daughter of Congressman Ebenezer Hill of Connecticut and chair of the College Women's Section of the parade. Each of these women played a key role in the events of March 3. Nina Allender was one of many who would follow Paul into the National Woman's Party and become the chief artist and cartoonist for *The Suffragist*.

PHOTOGRAPHS 7 AND 8 (*left and facing page*): One of the chief ways the suffragists had for advertising the parade was standing on the street and selling or giving away literature about suffrage and the parade. These pictures were taken by the Harris and Ewing photo service and published in the *Washington Post* on February 7, 1913. Photograph 7 shows (*left to right*) Mrs. Leslie Street, Lucy Burns, Jane Burleson, Mrs. Walter Thompson, and Marguerite Gove.

PHOTOGRAPH 9: Alice Paul became famous for her whirlwind efforts during January and February of 1913, and for her hat, which became a symbol of those efforts. It was said that she stayed too busy to take off her hat. The other woman in this picture is not identified but may be Helena Hill Weed, daughter of Congressman Ebenezer Hill of Connecticut.

PHOTOGRAPH 10: The biggest contribution that NAWSA made to Paul's efforts was certainly not money. The leadership had given her an annual budget of ten dollars and repeatedly made it clear that NAWSA would not bear any of the costs of the parade. NAWSA constantly harassed Paul about how much money she was spending. They did give her the services of Helen Gardner, who handled press relations for the parade committee. Gardner sent out a constant stream of press releases and other information that kept journalists interested and attentive.

PHOTOGRAPH 11 (*facing page*): New York socialite Elizabeth Rogers volunteered to help the parade committee in its efforts to publicize the event by becoming one of its public speakers. She was married to a distinguished New York physician, but she was more valuable because of another family conection. Her brother-in-law was Henry Stimson, secretary of war in the outgoing Taft administration. Paul asked Rogers to appeal to Stimson to provide the marchers with protection by the U.S. Army. At first Stimson refused but then reconsidered and ordered the Fifteenth Cavalry to be ready to respond if there was trouble. That they did.

PHOTOGRAPH 12: Public speaking events were a central and almost daily part of Paul's plans to publicize the parade and the cause of suffrage. Some collections identify the woman speaking in this photo as Mary Beard. The *Washington Post* printed the picture on February 7 and identified her as Mrs. Glendower Evans of Boston.

PHOTOGRAPH 13: One of the most visually striking things about the parade was the number of women on horseback. They were organized by Genevieve Wimsatt, daughter of a wealthy Washington-area family. This photo appeared in the parade program and thus was not taken at the time of the parade.

The Photographs

PHOTOGRAPH 14: The Congressional Committee of NAWSA did not have a physical headquarters when Paul arrived in Washington in December. Paul contracted to rent this cramped basement location at 1420 F Street for sixty dollars a month. The space had its advantages, however. It was in the heart of the city and near the famous Woodward & Lothrop Department Store ("Woodies" to Washingtonians) and was in the view of thousands of people every day.

PHOTOGRAPH 15: Richard Sylvester, the chief of the Washington, D.C., police, served as the suffragists' nemesis throughout the story of the suffrage parade. He first refused them a permit to march on Pennsylvania Avenue. Then he tried to persuade them to hold their march elsewhere and at another time. Sylvester always expressed sympathy with the cause of suffrage, but his actions sent another message to his police force. Sylvester and his force became the villains of the suffrage parade fiasco, and his reputation never recovered. He was dismissed as police chief in 1915.

PHOTOGRAPH 16: The parade committee produced an elaborate twenty-page program that gave detailed information about many of the women who were involved with planning the event. The program, edited by Harriot Connor Brown, outlined the purpose of the event and included a description of the order of the procession with a list of what delegations and floats were in each section. There was also a chronology of the pageant planned for the plaza of the U.S. Treasury building. The colors on the cover are predominantly purple and yellow, and the women in the drawing strike heroic poses.

The Suffrage Hikers

New York socialite Rosalie Jones generated enormous publicity for the cause of suffrage in New York in December by leading a group of women on a "hike" from New York City to Albany. In January she announced—with the blessing of NAWSA but not Alice Paul—that she would do the same thing for the Washington suffrage parade. This audacious stunt would have a group of women hiking through the February weather of New Jersey, Delaware, and Maryland to join the women from the rest of the country in a giant procession for a federal suffrage amendment. Journalists loved it. The hike drew great crowds and much press coverage as it proceeded southward, and by the time the group reached Washington, Jones had become one of the stars of the show. Many people attended the parade on March 3 in great part to see the self-appointed "General" Jones and her army of hikers.

PHOTOGRAPH 17: Two days before the hikers left New York City, they began their publicity campaign by climbing atop an open-air bus on Fifth Avenue to take pictures, circulate literature, make a lot of noise, and collect funds for their cause.

PHOTOGRAPHS 18 AND 19 (*facing page*): The hike began on February 12 and would last for sixteen days. Wherever the hikers went, they attracted crowds of people and journalists. Since Rosalie Jones had dubbed herself a "general," the journalists referred to themselves as "war correspondents." These photos were probably taken in Newark, New Jersey, on the first or second day of the hike.

PHOTOGRAPH 20: The hike was not an easy trek, despite the enthusiasm of the crowds along the way. The weather was often cold and sometimes snowy. But most of the hikers endured and remained in good spirits. The hike was not all smiles and enthusiasm. A couple of days before the hikers reached Washington, a report surfaced that a band of African American women wanted to join the hikers as they came through Maryland and into the District. The *Washington Post,* in reporting on the incident in the February 27 edition, said Rosalie Jones promised that, if "colored women" joined the group, it would be "summarily disbanded" and the pilgrims would take trains either for New York or Washington.

PHOTOGRAPHS 21 AND 22 (*facing page*): Rosalie Jones had loudly proclaimed that, once in Washington, she and the hikers would deliver a letter to the newly elected president in the White House. The NAWSA leadership had second thoughts about having Jones represent the cause of suffrage to the new president, and the day before they reached the District of Columbia, they dispatched Alice Paul to relieve Jones of the letter. Jones angrily gave it to Paul and told the journalists what had happened. Once the controversy went public, the NAWSA leadership backed off and assured Jones she would be able to see Wilson. It was a brouhaha that soured relations between Paul and Jones. The hikers arrived in the District (with no "colored women" as part of their group) on Friday, February 28. The many news stories that had been printed about them already had made them famous, and they began to draw a large crowd as they walked down Pennsylvania Avenue toward their hotel. Note that, at the lower right of Photograph 22, a movie camera is set up to capture the moments.

PHOTOGRAPHS 23 AND 24: The parade committee welcomed the hikers with a mounted escort, which led them to their hotel. The escort undoubtedly added to the festive atmosphere of the arrival and was something of a small precursor to the parade that would occur the following Monday.

PHOTOGRAPHS 25 AND 26: Part of the escort the hikers received was an automobile carrying the chairman of the parade committee, Alice Paul. At some point, Jones was presented with a bouquet of flowers and joined Paul in the automobile. Both women can be seen at the lower part of Photograph 25 (*above*) as they arrive at the hotel. Photograph 26 (*right*) must have been taken shortly after that arrival.

PHOTOGRAPH 27: The enormity of the crowd that surrounded the hikers, evident in Photograph 27, set off alarm bells for Alice Paul. The District police were not able to handle all of these people and keep the streets clear for this small band of marchers. What would the situation be on Monday? Much of Paul's efforts that weekend before the parade were directed at ensuring the security and safety of the marchers on Monday.

Before the Parade

The parade was not scheduled to begin until 3 p.m. on that Monday. One of the advantages of the mid-afternoon start was to give out-of-town marchers much of the day to arrive in Washington. As they came in to Union Station and other points in the city, they were directed to the areas on the west and south sides of the U.S. Capitol building. The head of the parade would form at the Garfield Monument and then move toward the Peace Monument and then onto Pennsylvania Avenue. The hour or two before the parade provided an excellent time for photographers to take pictures of the parade participants. Since the parade was not in progress, the marchers could stand still for the cameras. Unfortunately, most of the photographers seemed to concentrate on the beginning of the parade rather than lugging their bulky cameras around to the south of the Capitol to capture the other participants. Photojournalists of the day were also not attuned to keeping specific records of what they shot, so we do not always know everyone who appears in the picture. Still, to look at these pictures in their entirety is to get a sense of the excitement and anticipation everyone must have felt during those moments before the parade began.

PHOTOGRAPHS 28 AND 29 (*left and below left*): Inez Milholland drew a crowd even before the parade began. Her dark hair and light-colored robes and horse were a striking contrast of colors and light. People wanted to see her up close, and it appears from these photos that many people, particularly men, wanted to be in the photographs with her. Note the African American groom in Photos 28 and 30. His name has been lost to us, but he apparently stayed with her and her horse, "Grey Dawn," throughout the parade. In each of these photographs, Milholland seems to be enjoying herself and her starring role immensely.

PHOTOGRAPH 30: In its story about the parade on March 4, the *Washington Post* called Inez Milholland "by far the most picturesque figure in the parade." It was an accolade she had become used to receiving.

PHOTOGRAPHS 31, 32, AND 33: The parade's grand marshal, Jane Burleson, was the center of attention for many of the photographers as participants in the parade began to gather around the base of Capitol Hill that afternoon. In Photo 31 (*left*), she is standing with (*left to right*) Mary Blair (*holding the muff*), Mrs. W. Albert Wood, Burleson (*in the middle*), and Dr. and Mrs. O. J. Stevenson. The man on the extreme left is not identified. Photo 32 (*below left*) shows Blair, Wood, and Burleson, with Stevenson in the background. Photo 33 (*below right*) shows Burleson handing out something—possibly sashes—from a box to some of the parade marshals. In each of these photos, Burleson has on a different hat than the one she wore in the parade.

PHOTOGRAPH 34: Burleson is standing third from the right along with parade marshals (*left to right*) Mrs. Russell McLennan, Althea Taft, Louise Bridges Alberta Hill, and Miss F. Ragsdale. The women appear to be relaxed and enjoying themselves.

PHOTOGRAPH 35: Jane Burleson also cut a striking and impressive figure on a horse. As grand marshal, she led the first contingent of the parade and was charged with starting the procession. An artist from Texas, she was married to an Army lieutenant stationed at Ft. Myer near Washington. She was well known as a horsewoman in District social circles, and her beauty, equestrian abilities, and confidence are evident in these photographs.

PHOTOGRAPH 36: Parade marshal Alberta Hill is shown mounted on her horse. She was one of the mounted aides that accompanied Jane Burleson, who was leading the parade.

PHOTOGRAPHS 37 AND 38: None of these mounted marshals in these two photos is specifically identified. The women in Photo 37 (*left*) are dressed in light colors and riding light-colored horses. The *New York Times* story on March 4 about the parade names "Mrs. Ruhlin, Mrs. Lucy Neill and Mrs. Merrill" as marshals wearing "white corduroy riding habits and wide-brimmed hats" may identify these three women. Note that they are riding side-saddle. The woman in Photo 38 (*above*) is astride the horse. She is holding a horn in her right hand, which means she is probably a herald for one of the sections of the parade.

PHOTOGRAPH 39: The Missouri Ladies Military Band of Marysville, Missouri, was a thirty-five-member band that traveled more than fifteen hundred miles to participate in the parade. The band wore blue uniforms. They are pictured marching in Photograph 57.

PHOTOGRAPH 40: One of the highlights of the parade was the focus on countries that had made more progress toward women's suffrage than the United States. In fact, these groups were part of the first section of the parade. This photo is a group of women from Sweden, where women had obtained partial suffrage.

The Photographs

PHOTOGRAPHS 41 AND 42: The most photographed float of the March 3 parade was the Women of the Bible Lands float. It was elaborate and crowded with women representing the biblical characters Deborah, Miriam, Huldah, and the four daughters of the evangelist Philip. Note in Photo 42 (*right*) the African American child in the center of the float, partially hidden by the flagpole.

PHOTOGRAPH 43: Mrs. Woodward Clark stands atop the Australia float. Australia is one of the countries where women had already achieved full suffrage.

PHOTOGRAPH 44: This group of women represented homemakers and was part of the third section of the parade. They are moving quickly, and they appear to be having a lot of fun. An important argument that suffragists had to make again and again was that women would not abandon the home if they were given the right to vote. This group was given a prominent position in the parade.

PHOTOGRAPH 45: Mrs. Raymond Brown, president of the New York Suffrage Association, was one of a large number of New York women who attended the parade. These women represented not only the state association but also the National American Woman Suffrage Association and the Women's Political Union.

PHOTOGRAPHS 46 AND 47: Delegations of women from almost every state in the union were represented in the parade. These photos show parts of two delegations from the South, Louisiana and Georgia. They were of particular concern to Alice Paul when a group from Howard University in Washington, D.C., wanted to join the parade. Paul feared that the racism of the southern white women would prevent them from supporting the parade if the group from Howard was allowed to join. Her fears were likely justified, but racial prejudice was not confined to the South. It was embedded in the entire country, as illustrated by the reaction of Rosalie Jones to the idea that suffrage hikers might be accompanied into Washington by a band of "colored women." (See caption to Photograph 20.)

The Photographs

PHOTOGRAPH 48: Harriet Taylor Upton of Ohio is shown with the leaders of other state delegations. Upton was a prominent suffragist and remained so through the rest of the decade. She was in Nashville in August 1920 when the Nineteenth Amendment was passed by the Tennessee legislature—the final legislative move that ratified the amendment and gave women the right to vote.

PHOTOGRAPH 49: Grace Wilbur Trout, president of the Illinois Suffrage Association, led a delegation from that state to Washington for the parade. They traveled by train on a "manless special," according to the *New York Times* (March 3, 1913, p. 7). The train carried a hundred women and derived its nickname from the fact that women served as porters. At stops along the way, the women made speeches and "sometimes they poured tea for visitors."

PHOTOGRAPH 50: Women from every part of the nation came to Washington for the parade. These two unidentified women from Iowa traveled nearly 2,000 miles to attend the parade. Their faces and demeanors attest to this being indeed a proud moment for them.

The Photographs

Upper Pennsylvania Avenue before the Parade

Police had strung rope barriers along the curbs on the most of the parade route, but they had not stopped traffic or streetcars from coming through the area until that afternoon. Police Chief Richard Sylvester said he did not have the authority to do so. For two months, dozens of women had worked almost nonstop to publicize the parade, and newspapers had been full of stories about the parade, the hikers, the colorful floats, the pageant—along with the fact that the Wilson inaugural ceremonies the next day would be minimal. By early afternoon, the crowds gathering in the Pennsylvania Avenue–Fourteenth Street area were massive, as the pictures in this section show. In none of these photos do the people look packed or uncomfortable. Nor do they look hostile. There are plenty of women and children to be found. But it is clear that they are not going to fit on the curbs of the avenue.

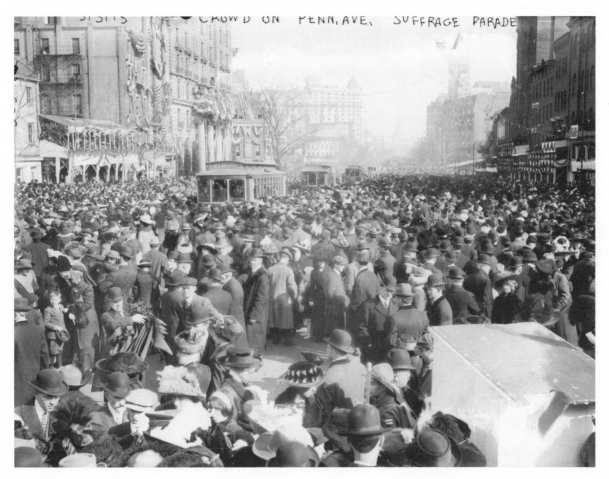

PHOTOGRAPHS 51 AND 52: Each of these pictures shows the area at a different time and different angle, but they confirm that there was a huge crowd of people that stretched far down the middle of Pennsylvania Avenue. Even under the best of circumstances, the participants would have had difficulty in getting through this area and over to the Treasury building.

PHOTOGRAPH 53: The head of the parade had formed on the west side of the Capitol building, and as it moved forward, it turned left onto Pennsylvania Avenue. Jane Burleson and her attendants were first, followed by the herald, Inez Mulholland (the white figure at the base of the Peace Monument). A sign stating a demand for a federal suffrage amendment (behind the flag bearer on the right) was mounted on a wagon behind Mulholland. Then came the light-colored mounted marshals. Burleson moved up the avenue for a few yards and then stopped to see that everyone was moving behind her. A photographer on the right is taking a picture of this moment. Two more photographers stand between the streetcar tracks closer to Milholland. Note the policeman on the left side.

The Photographs

Starting the Parade

Sometime around 3:20 p.m., Jane Burleson gave the signal, and the parade began to move. Pennsylvania Avenue was not clear. That was apparent to anyone who was at the Peace Monument, particularly to anyone who was on a horse and could see up the avenue. But the marchers and the crowd could not wait any longer. They had to start, despite the uncertainty of what lay ahead.

PHOTOGRAPH 54: Inez Milholland shows what a striking and eye-catching part of the parade she was as she rides in the first block of Pennsylvania Avenue, followed by the mounted sign demanding a federal suffrage amendment. The African American groom for her horse, "Grey Dawn," walks beside her in case he is needed to calm the horse in front of the large crowd.

PHOTOGRAPH 55: This set of ushers, clad in light blue capes and bonnets trimmed with gold, marched some yards behind the sign and the plumed marshals on their white horses. (See Photograph 54.) They immediately preceded the officers of NAWSA, the nominal sponsoring organization of the parade. The woman in the dark graduation gown seen between two of the ushers on the right is likely Dr. Anna Howard Shaw, the president of NAWSA.

PHOTOGRAPH 56: As part of the first section of the parade, these women from countries where women had been given partial suffrage made an important point. They wanted to show Americans that other countries had moved forward in granting political rights to women. Again, note the photographers on the right.

The Photographs

PHOTOGRAPH 57: The Missouri Ladies Military Band of Marysville, Missouri, gets to show off its marching and musical talents to the growing crowd of onlookers. (See Photograph 39.)

PHOTOGRAPH 58: It is not clear which delegation of women appears in this photograph, which is rounding the circle of the Peace Monument and coming onto Pennsylvania Avenue. A policeman looks on at the far right. The designation on the photograph made by the photographer or photo editor uses the word "suffragette," a term that most American suffragists avoided because of its association with militant British suffragists.

The Photographs

PHOTOGRAPH 59: The delegation of home-makers, seen in Photograph 44, makes its way past the first intersection on Pennsylvania. They follow a float titled "In the Home." On the far right, a photographer walks back toward the Peace Monument.

PHOTOGRAPH 60: The delegations of college women in section three of the parade were large and impressive. The *Washington Post* estimated the number of graduates to be one thousand. The delegations in the photograph are from Bryn Mawr, Vassar, and Wellesley. Alice Paul had hoped to be part of the Swarthmore contingent, but by this time she was in a car far up Pennsylvania Avenue, trying to clear a path for the marchers.

The Photographs

PHOTOGRAPH 61: These nurses were part of the third section, which included farmers, homemakers, college women, lawyers, doctors, pharmacists, and "wage-earners." Here, in the first block of the parade, the lines are straight and orderly.

PHOTOGRAPH 62: The official procession program notes that the biblical float "was arranged by Madame Lydia Von F. Mountford of Jerusalem, and the characters shown on it were dressed in costumes taken from her collection donated to the American University. Mmd. Mountford says that women in Bible lands who hold property in real estate vote in local affairs."

The Pageant

At the other end of Pennsylvania Avenue, on the plaza of the U.S. Treasury building, the much anticipated pageant began at the same time as the parade. The overall pageant had been designed by Hazel MacKaye, and Florence Fleming Noyes arranged the dances for the allegory. The parade program summarized the pageant narrative this way: "Columbia, hearing the approach of the Procession, summons to her side Justice, Charity, Liberty, Peace and Hope, to review with her this 'new crusade' of women. When these are assembled, Columbia takes her place as leader and guardian of them all, and, in a final tableau, they stand together and review the oncoming Procession."

PHOTOGRAPH 63: Columbia, played by Hedwig Reicher, appears as the heralding trumpets sound.

PHOTOGRAPHS 64 AND 65: After the "Star Spangled Banner" is played, Columbia summons Justice, who appears with her attendants in purple and violet robes.

PHOTOGRAPHS 66 AND 67: Charity, in blue, and her attendants are then called forth.

PHOTOGRAPHS 68 AND 69: Liberty then comes forward to the sounds of the "Triumphal March" from *Aida*. Photograph 68 (*left*) appeared on the front page of the *Washington Post* on the day after the parade.

The Photographs

PHOTOGRAPHS 70 AND 71: Peace then appears between the columns of the building. Before descending the stairs, she releases a dove. She is then followed by Plenty.

PHOTOGRAPHS 72 AND 73:
The final summoning is to Hope
and her attendants.

PHOTOGRAPHS 74 AND 75: At the end of the pageant, Columbia and the entire troupe move forward to await the passing of the parade, which had been timed to happen at any moment. The parade made only halting progress along Pennsylvania Avenue. The women in the allegory waited for as long as they could stand it, but the chill air and the marble on their bare feet drove them inside the Treasury building.

PHOTOGRAPHS 76 AND 77: After a delay of more than an hour and a half, the troupe returned when they heard that the head of the parade was approaching.

The Struggle up Pennsylvania Avenue

The head of the parade ran into trouble with its procession at somewhere between Fourth and Fifth streets along Pennsylvania Avenue. The spectators had spilled into the streets, and there seemed little that the police could or would do at that point. Alice Paul and District officials were in cars that drove up the avenue ahead and on each side of the marchers, trying to clear a path. The cars did little good, however. People would move to avoid the cars but then surge back into place once the cars had passed. The lack of police, or their indifference in many locations, gave license to those who felt like disrupting the marchers.

Crowd braking parade up at 9th St · Mch 3 1913

PHOTOGRAPH 78: This photograph (*left*) was taken from the top of the Evening News Building looking back down Pennsylvania Avenue toward the U.S. Capitol. While few details can be seen, the crowds all along Pennsylvania Avenue are enormous and spilling well into the street at many points. The photo was taken at 4:15 p.m., a time when the parade should have been nearly over. Instead, it is still stretched all along the avenue.

PHOTOGRAPH 79: At Ninth Street the crowd was thick enough to break up the parade. Some in the crowd deliberately tried to interfere with the marchers, as is apparently happening here.

PHOTOGRAPH 80: At some points along Pennsylvania Avenue, marchers enjoyed a fairly wide berth and were unencumbered by the crowds. This float is at the end of section one and showcases costumed women representing countries that have active suffrage movements, such as Turkey, Persia, and Italy. It is followed by the Women of Bible Lands float. Note the Boy Scout at the far left of the photo holding the crowd back with a staff.

PHOTOGRAPH 81: The parade route had the marchers coming up Pennsylvania Avenue and turning left at Fourteenth Street toward the Treasury building (toward the right in this and other photos). This photo (*above*), taken from Fifteenth Street, shows Jane Burleson leading the parade almost to that point. Onlookers have crowded well onto Pennsylvania Avenue here, and even though the marchers have some room, the space for their ranks is obviously reduced.

PHOTOGRAPH 82: At the point where the parade is turning, those at the head of the parade were met by members of the Fifteenth Cavalry from Fort Myers, who have been dispatched to clear Pennsylvania Avenue. At the center are a cavalryman and Inez Milholland, the parade's herald.

11940—Suffragette Parade. Grand Marshall, Mrs. Richard Burleson; Herald, Miss Inez Milholland ; and other prominent workers on horseback—March 3, 1913, Washington, D. C.

PHOTOGRAPH 83: The parade is turning at this point with the sign demanding a suffrage amendment clearly visible. Milholland is at the far right of the photograph, and the top of one of the District's scout cars is in the middle. The crowd has become more densely packed because of the work of the Fifteenth Cavalry.

Suffrets Parade 1913
Was. D.C.

PHOTOGRAPH 84: At the center of the photo (*above left*), a cavalryman works to push the crowd back as one of the floats passes by. This is the point at which the parade turns, and there appears to be room for the participants, but the people in the crowd are tightly packed together.

PHOTOGRAPH 85: This photo taken from the same spot as Photograph 83 (*above right*) and shows both cavalry and police on horseback working to move the crowd back and having some success because the street pavement can be seen. The vehicle is one of the District of Columbia officials' scout cars that had been unsuccessful in clearing the crowd earlier.

PHOTOGRAPH 86: Back down Pennsylvania Avenue, at the intersection of E Street, the cavalry still had some work to do in moving the crowds back from the marchers.

The Photographs

Suf Parade 1913

PHOTOGRAPH 87: By the time the delegations of college graduates arrive at the E Street intersection, the crowds have been moved back so that the women can maintain their ranks.

PHOTOGRAPH 88: By the time section three, with the college delegations, had reached Fourteenth Street and the turn toward the Treasury building, the cavalry had succeeded in widening the amount of space along Pennsylvania Avenue for the marchers. The ranks of the college graduates are straight and unbroken.

PHOTOGRAPH 89: Once the entire parade had passed, onlookers again crowded onto Pennsylvania Avenue, making it difficult for ambulances to get to those who had been injured in the melees during the parade.

The End of the Parade

The Woman Suffrage Procession ended as it passed the reviewing stand in front of the Treasury building with the cast of the pageant looking on. The way had been cleared by the Fifteenth Cavalry, and there were no incidents at this stage. Some of the spectators, tired of waiting, had left the area, but there was still a large and enthusiastic crowd to greet the marchers, who had been through an eventful, frustrating, and sometimes difficult two hours. The photos of this portion of the parade show an attentive audience and a strong police presence.

PHOTOGRAPH 90: Jane Burleson leads her unit of mounted marshals past the reviewing stand across from the plaza of the Treasury building, the final point in the parade. Burleson and her troop were about an hour later in getting to this point than they had planned because of the enormous crowds along Pennsylvania Avenue. They are being watched from the vantage point of the photographer by the troop of the pageant, who had been waiting for them inside the Treasury building.

PHOTOGRAPH 91: Herald Inez Milholland wore a broad smile as she passed the reviewing stand. Mulholland seems to be enjoying herself here as she did in other parts of the parade.

PHOTOGRAPH 92: The first float of the parade, a sign demanding a federal suffrage amendment to the U.S. Constitution, passes by the reviewing stand accompanied by the plumed marshals.

PHOTOGRAPH 93: The Women of Bible Lands float, consistently a photographer's favorite among the units of the parade, passed by the reviewing stand with all of the original participants aboard and intact, despite the crowds on Pennsylvania Avenue.

PHOTOGRAPH 94: Many of these marchers, including this delegation of nurses, maintained their ranks at the end of the parade. Some of participants look understandably weary. Abby Scott Baker, who had been a marshal in the first part of the parade and who had such trouble getting to this point, later testified as to what a relief it was to see the open space in front of the Treasury building, which she attributed to the soldiers of the Fifteenth Cavalry: "I just saw them standing and was thankful to see them there."

PHOTOGRAPH 95: Another of the parade's floats passes by the reviewing stand across from the Treasury building plaza. Note the Boy Scout at the far left.

Woodrow Wilson's Arrival and Inaugural

Shortly after the parade began, Woodrow Wilson arrived in Washington, D.C., by train at Union Station. The journey had begun at Princeton, New Jersey, Wilson's residence, earlier that day, and the train bore many of Wilson's friends and supporters.

PHOTOGRAPH 96: A large, though not overwhelming, crowd was on hand to greet the president-elect as his train pulled into Union Station. In this photo Wilson leaves the station amid a cast of dignitaries. The uniformed man on the right between two civilians is probably Police Chief Richard Sylvester.

PHOTOGRAPHS 97 AND 98: The inaugural parade for Woodrow Wilson on March 4 was dignified and simple, as promised. It came off without incident.

The Aftermath

Shortly after the Washington Suffrage Parade began on the afternoon of March 3, 1913, President-elect Woodrow Wilson alighted from the train that brought him from Princeton, New Jersey. Looking around, the story goes, Wilson asked, slightly peeved and somewhat disappointed, "Where are the people?" An aide (or someone) responds, "On the Avenue, watching the suffragists parade."[1]

The story may or may not be true. Several hundred people accompanied Wilson on his journey from Princeton, and there were approximately five thousand (according to the *New-York Tribune*) at Union Station to greet him on his arrival.[2] Whatever his expectations were, it is unlikely that he noticed—or cared—that a more massive number of people were not on hand.

Wilson was loudly cheered when he walked out of the station and taken to his hotel by a circuitous route to avoid the crowds gathered around Pennsylvania Avenue. Wilson never saw any part of the parade and, as far as we know, never made any substantive public comment about it. Suffrage was not an issue that he had given much thought to and not one that he believed merited much of his consideration.

But to some suffragists—Alice Paul, particularly—the president-elect was the single most significant target of her efforts on March 3. If anyone could make suffrage happen quickly, it was the president of the United States. And on March 4, that person would be Woodrow Wilson. Getting the president's attention would be the chief focus of her efforts during the next seven years.

The cause of suffrage received a significant boost from the events of March 3, 1913. Millions of people either saw or read about the march itself. When the Senate investigation began later that week and continued through the month, millions more would become aware of the issue. The women who participated in the march, and those who wished to, found a new sense of purpose and resolve in trying to gain the right to vote.

While millions of Americans—probably a majority—still held to the notion that women had no business in the voting booth, the idea of suffrage had been launched past the "ridicule stage" that Alice Paul had identified three years earlier when she returned from England. Suffrage was gaining adherents and would have to be taken seriously.

But for those participants and spectators who left Pennsylvania Avenue that evening thinking that a national suffrage amendment was just around the corner, there was disappointment ahead. The parade itself could serve as a metaphor for what happened to the federal amendment over the next seven years. There were starts and stops and long, frustrating periods of time spent waiting. There were the catcallers and hecklers and even those who tried to take down the banners. There were people the suffragists counted on who did not deliver as promised. There was glacially slow movement. Finally, there was a clear path and eventual victory. But it all took far longer than suffragists believed necessary.

Even after the parade and its immediate aftermath, many suffragists were not convinced that major efforts should be made in trying to pass a federal amendment. Some of this belief was simply adherence to the longtime state-by-state strategy of NAWSA. The parade was helpful to suffrage efforts in some states, they believed, but trying to get a federal amendment would be futile.

Another contingent of the state-by-staters was ideological. There *should not* be a federal amendment, they thought. Voting laws were in the privilege of the states, not the federal government. This was the view of Kate Gordon, a Louisiana suffragist, who formed the Southern States Woman Suffrage Conference to lobby state legislatures for the right to vote. Many of these women believed that a federal suffrage amendment would destroy the carefully constructed voting laws that kept most southern African Americans away from the polls. States, they thought, should be able to make laws that allowed only white women to vote, not black women.

But the parade had clarified the suffrage issue and simplified the strategy for many others, which is what Paul and her cohorts had intended. A federal amendment was the only way and the inevitable way.

The suffrage amendment, as usual, was introduced in the Congressional session in 1913 and received some attention from legislators but did not get out of committee and onto the Senate floor for a vote until the next year, when it was defeated. Meanwhile, Illinois granted women partial suffrage—the right to vote in presidential elections. In 1914 Nevada and Montana voted in full suffrage for women.

Within the suffrage movement, all was not well. Alice Paul had demonstrated her independence from NAWSA by forming the Congressional Union, which was the fundraising arm of the Congressional Committee that she and Burns had been appointed to lead. The CU was necessary because expenses for the parade far exceeded the ten dollars NAWSA had given them to operate in 1913. When Paul delivered her report to NAWSA in December 1913, an inquiry ensued as to why the CU's money had not gone into the NAWSA treasury. Paul refused to allow the CU to become part of NAWSA, which precipitated a separation by Paul and her adherents and the formation of the National Woman's

Party. The break with the conservative leadership of the mother organization allowed Paul and her cohorts to adopt the strategy of her British mentors by holding the party in power—the president and the Democrats—responsible for the lack of suffrage. It was a strategy that NAWSA could never consider.

Many of NAWSA's members did not want to abandon the organization but recognized that it could not continue down the same path. In 1915 Carrie Chapman Catt replaced Anna Howard Shaw as president. Catt not only brought organizational coherence to NAWSA (something Shaw had never been able to do) but also began to shift its focus toward a federal amendment.

At the same time, Catt and Paul attempted a reconciliation, but the gulf between the personalities, the organizations, and their strategies was too wide to bridge. Paul continued to believe that public attention was best for the cause of suffrage; Catt stuck with quiet persuasion. Both undoubtedly recognized the strengths of this dual approach, but they remained at odds with one another until the very last stages of the suffrage debate.

Paul announced that the National Woman's Party (the successor to her Congressional Union) would send teams of campaigners into selected states to campaign against Democrats in the 1916 elections—even when the individual Democrats they were trying to defeat happened to be pro-suffrage. Her message was that suffrage could be a reality quickly if Wilson and his party would simply enact it.

Paul and the NWP did not succeed in ousting Wilson or the Democrats in 1916—they claimed a few victories but overall their impact was light—but suffrage had moved up appreciably on the national political agenda. The Democratic Party had a pro-suffrage plank, a rather tepid one, in its platform, and the federal amendment was endorsed fully by Republican presidential nominee Charles Evans Hughes. The Republicans came closer to defeating Wilson than anyone had expected, although few attributed Hughes's stand on suffrage as affecting the outcome of the election.

In January 1917, with Wilson back in the White House for another four years, th'
campaign to keep suffrage in the public eye—picketing the White House. On Janu'
stationed themselves in front of the entrance to the White House. They held banners den
and demanding that Wilson act immediately. They did not move, and they said nothing ι
from bystanders and journalists. Nothing like this had ever been done before.

As with the suffrage parade in 1913, these "silent sentinels" (a concept within Paul's Quaker
a strong reaction and a desire to join in among women hoping for the right to vote and wanting to do sι
it. Over the next two months, hundreds came to Washington to participate in these daily demonstrations.
silently through rain and cold, once refusing the president's offer to come inside the White House for a warm cι

Wilson's second inauguration, in March 1917, provoked another suffrage demonstration. In this one, ι
members braved the rain of inauguration day and marched around the White House holding banners demanding tha,
Wilson support a suffrage amendment. But American politics has been invaded by a foreign policy issue that would
engulf everything in its path—the ongoing war in Europe. By this time, Germany's continue aggression on the seas had
made Wilson's neutrality untenable for the president, and on April 2, Wilson asked Congress for a declaration of war.[3]

The war opened an even wider gulf in the suffrage movement. Catt, even though a strong pacifist, announced
that NAWSA would suspend its lobbying for suffrage and participate in the war efforts. Paul and the NWP said the opposite. It would continue its picketing and discourage women from supporting the war until women had the franchise.
Why should women support something like a war in which they had no voice in deciding, she asked?[4]

Paul's pickets continued to stand in front of the White House, and while they remained silent, their signs
grew more pointed. They began quoting the president's own words about democracy as a justification for America's

ation in the war. Their signs provoked predict-
actions from those who feel that dissent during
ime is traitorous. The picketers were set upon by
ry crowds, and eventually, instead of being pro-
cted by the police, they were arrested.[5]

For those familiar with what had happened in
Britain a decade earlier (and Paul certainly was), the
drama was predictable. The women were defiant in
court. They were sentenced to jail. They demanded political status as prisoners and refused to wear prison
clothing. They went on a hunger strike. They were force-
fed. When finally released, they were treated as heroes.
This happened again and again over the next months.

Catt, working within the administration, hoped
the Wilson administration would include suffrage as
part of the war measure presented to Congress. That did
not happen, but the suffrage political train was picking
up some stream. In late 1917 New York became the first
eastern state to vote in a full suffrage amendment to its
constitution. Other states gave women the right to vote

Virginia Arnold, a member of the National Woman's Party, stands in
front of the White House with a sign excoriating Woodrow Wilson. The
photo was taken in August 1917, four months after the United States
had entered the war against Germany. Arnold and many other women—
including Alice Paul and Lucy Burns—were arrested. They were charged
with "obstructing sidewalk traffic." (Library of Congress.)

in presidential elections. In 1918 Wilson publicly endorsed a federal amendment and made a special address to Congress on the issue, but the amendment still failed to gain the necessary two-thirds majorities it needed.

Paul and her adherents continued to hold public demonstrations and still held the president responsible for the lack of suffrage. Despite his public declarations of support, she said, he was not doing enough to persuade legislators to vote for it.

Finally, in June 1919, after many frustrating delays, debates, and votes, the Nineteenth Amendment passed both houses of Congress and was sent to the states for ratification. Three-fourths of the states, thirty-six out of forty-eight, were necessary to have the amendment entered into the Constitution, and those thirty-six did not come easily.

Ratification became a race with the clock as suffragists wanted the right to vote by the 1920 presidential election in November and each party sought to take credit for it and reap what it thought might be the amendment's election benefits. But opponents of suffrage were still alive, well entrenched, and willing to fight. The arguments they made were racial (African American voting could no longer be controlled), states' rights (states should have the sole power to enact voting laws), and traditional (enfranchising women would destroy homes and dilute the good influence of women).

By late spring of 1920, thirty-five states had ratified the amendment and eight states had rejected it. Of the five that were left, the prospects for passage were not good, or the legislative sessions were over and the governors were not inclined to call the legislators back. The only possibility was Tennessee. There, the governor—a pro-Wilson man—responded positively to an appeal by the president and called the legislature back into session in August.

For three weeks that hot summer, Nashville hosted a circus of pro- and anti-suffragist supporters and events. All of the forces on either side of the issue gathered, and all of the arguments were presented in a variety of forums.[6]

When the legislature finally went into session, the Senate passed the amendment quickly and decisively. After nearly a week of debating and lobbying, the House also passed the ratification motion—by a single vote.[7]

The changes wrought by the Nineteenth Amendment were not sudden or dramatic. The Republicans won the 1920 elections, and there is little evidence that women voting made much difference.

But the passage of the Nineteenth Amendment was the most profound shift in the electorate in the history of the Republic. In one stroke, millions of people who had never had the ballot before suddenly had a voice. Politicians, who once could dismiss them without fear of reprisal, now had to pay attention. Issues that could be safely ignored or put aside gained new life. New political organizations and processes would take shape.

Most importantly, Americans developed a new way of thinking about their politics, about the structure of their society, and about themselves.

Notes

1. Doris Stevens, *Jailed for Freedom: American Women Win the Vote* (1920; rev. ed., Troutdale, OR: New Sage Press, 1995), 35. Stevens wasn't there and doesn't attribute the story to any source. Nevertheless, the story is repeated by Inez Irwin in *Up Hill with Banners Flying* (Penobscot, ME: Traversity Press, 1964), 31, without citation. Stevens is cited for this story by Walton in *A Woman's Crusade*, 74.

2. "Wilson ready to take oath; cabinet picked" (*New-York Tribune*, March 4, 1913, http://proxy. lib.utk.edu/docview/575063541?accountid=14766.

3. Jeanette Rankin, the first female member of Congress, had been elected to represent the Second District of Montana the previous November. She was one of fifty members of the House of Representatives who voted against the declaration of war. Twenty-four years later, in 1941, Rankin was again serving in Congress when President Franklin Roosevelt asked Congress to declare war against Japan. An avowed pacifist, Rankin again voted no, making her the only member of Congress to vote against America entering both world wars.

4. In 1914, Emmeline Pankhurst had taken the same route as Catt in suspending suffrage work in favor of supporting Great Britain's war effort. Before the war broke out, Pankhurst, too, had been an outspoken pacifist.

5. The Wilson administration's treatment of dissent during this time is an ugly chapter in America's history of civil liberties. What happened to the suffrage picketers was indeed gentle compare to what other jailed dissenters endured. Catt was so put out with what Paul and the NWP were

doing that she never raised her voice against the treatment the jailed suffragists received. In fact, she participated in a scheme of Wilson administration officials to try to persuade newspaper publishers to ignore the picketers. The scheme failed.

6. Catt came to Nashville and directed the lobbying efforts of the suffragists. Paul stayed in Washington but dispatched Tennessean Sue Shelton White as a representative of the National Woman's Party. Catt and White seemed to be cordial with one another and apparently worked cooperatively.

7. The full story of suffrage's final act in Nashville has yet to be fully researched and written. The decisive vote came from an East Tennessee Republican, Harry Burn, who was, at twenty-four, the youngest member of the House. Burn had been counted with the anti-suffrage forces during all the lobbying efforts and even voted with them on the motion to table the measure. That vote ended in a tie, which by parliamentary rules means that it failed. A vote on the measure itself was taken immediately afterwards. As the roll was being called alphabetically, Burn's name came up early, and his "aye" sent a delayed ripple through the chamber. It took at least a moment for observers to realize what had happened. The roll call continued, and the suffragists realized they were on the edge of victory. When the voting was concluded and the results announced, the suffragists broke out into cheers. Asked afterwards why he switched his vote, Burn produced a letter from his mother saying he should "help Mrs. Catt" if she needed him.

Epilogue

Most of the people who planned and participated in the Washington suffrage parade were young or in their middle years. For many of them, the parade was the first of many notable events in their lives. Life after the parade for some of the principals in this story is worth noting.

ALICE PAUL continued her fight for suffrage, eventually breaking with the National American Woman Suffrage Association and forming the National Woman's Party, the "militant wing" of the suffrage movement. She pioneered forms of public protest and inspired many of those who participated in the parade to follow her into the streets and eventually into prison. When the Nineteenth Amendment was ratified in 1920, she considered it only the first step toward a larger goal—complete legal equality for men and women. She continued to work toward that end. An equal rights amendment—the Alice Paul amendment—was passed by Congress in 1972, but the measure contained a seven-year ratification period. The amendment came within three states of being approved by the original deadline of 1979. A three-year extension for the amendment was passed, but it still failed to obtain the approval of enough states. Alice Paul died in 1977.

LUCY BURNS continued to work closely with Alice Paul during the next seven years of suffrage battles. She was jailed numerous times and endured many privations in prison, including force-feeding after leading a hunger strike for other prisoners. Once the Nineteenth Amendment was ratified, Burns left the movement with some bitter words for women who failed to participate in suffrage efforts but were now sharing in its benefits. She returned to Brooklyn, New York, where she lived until her death in 1966.

INEZ MILHOLLAND returned to New York after the parade and began her law practice, but she remained at the forefront of the suffrage movement. She was also part of other progressive causes, joining the National Association for the Advancement of Colored People at its inception. She was a dedicated pacifist and traveled to Italy during World War I as a correspondent for a Canadian newspaper, composing pacifist-oriented articles. Her writings irritated the Italian government and got her deported. She left NAWSA along with Paul and others and became part of the National Woman's Party. In 1916 she was recruited by Paul to go on a speaking tour in California, where the NWP was trying to defeat Democrats. During a speech in Los Angeles, she collapsed and died a month later of pernicious anemia. She was thirty years old. In death as in life, she became a symbol for the suffragists—the first martyr for their cause.

The conduct of the police in failing to plan for the crowd and protect the marchers ruined RICHARD SYLVESTER'S sterling reputation in law enforcement. He resigned as police chief in 1915 with the Washington Suffrage Parade still hanging over his head. He worked as the chief of police for du Pont in Delaware, a job that took on added significance when the United States joined World War I and the company began supplying vital war material. He was active and innovative in law enforcement internationally through the 1920s and retired in December 1930. He died two weeks after his retirement.

After leading the Washington Suffrage Parade, JANE BURLESON played almost no significant role in the suffrage movement. In 1936, her husband, an Army officer, divorced her, claiming she was interfering with his duties. In 1940, while living in her hometown of Galveston, Texas, she took a train to Charleston, South Carolina. Once there, she found the restaurant where the woman her husband had married was dining. Burleson shot and killed her. She pled insanity at her trial, was convicted of manslaughter, and served seven years in a South Carolina prison. She then returned to Galveston, where she lived until her death in 1957. As a convicted felon, she was not allowed to vote.

Index

Seeing Suffrage was designed and typeset on a Macintosh 10.6.8 computer system using InDesign CS5 software. The body text is set in 12/19.5 Kepler Std and display type is set in Bodoni Std Poster. This book was designed and typeset by Barbara Karwhite and manufactured by Thomson-Shore, Inc.